Van Nooten, B. A.
The Mahabharata

TWAYNE'S WORLD AUTHORS SERIES

A Survey of the World's Literature

Sylvia E. Bowman, Indiana University

GENERAL EDITOR

INDIA

Raul de L. Furtado

EDITOR

The Mahābhārata

(*TWAS 131*)

TWAYNE'S WORLD AUTHORS SERIES (TWAS)

The purpose of TWAS is to survey the major writers —novelists, dramatists, historians, poets, philosophers, and critics—of the nations of the world. Among the national literatures covered are those of Australia, Canada, China, Eastern Europe, France, Germany, Greece, India, Italy, Japan, Latin America, the Netherlands, New Zealand, Poland, Russia, Scandinavia, Spain, and the African nations, as well as Hebrew, Yiddish, and Latin Classical literatures. This survey is complemented by Twayne's United States Authors Series and English Authors Series

The intent of each volume in these series is to present a critical-analytical study of the works of the writer; to include biographical and historical material that may be necessary for understanding, appreciation, and critical appraisal of the writer; and to present all material in clear, concise English—but not to vitiate the scholarly content of the work by doing so.

The Mahābhārata

attributed to

Kṛṣṇa Dvaipāyana Vyāsa

By BAREND A. VAN NOOTEN

Twayne Publishers, Inc. :: New York

Library of Congress Catalog Card Number: 74-99543

MANUFACTURED IN THE UNITED STATES OF AMERICA

To my teacher, adviser, and friend

Murray Benson Emeneau

Preface

THE present work gives a description of the character and history of the Sanskrit literary work, the *Mahābhārata,* an epic with philosophical overtones. This gigantic work, the longest epic in the world, has in the two thousand years since its composition exerted an unparalleled influence on the culture and thinking of the people of India. In the mainstream of Indian cultural history, the *Mahābhārata* is like an undercurrent which surfaces now and then to appear in a new form, colored by the convictions and predilections of the period. Thanks to the encyclopedic character of its contents, it has become a source of inspiration for the most curiously diverse literary forms; philosophical, entertaining, religious, and erotic works have drawn on it for their themes and motives. It has been maligned by Buddhists and Jains, but the latter ultimately adopted it as a literary work of their own. Finally, the modern Hindu can trace many of his unconscious notions about good and evil, auspicious and ominous, back to this epic.

The *Mahābhārata* is not .easy to read, even in translation. This book aims at guiding the reader through the vast labyrinth of this epic, to show him its plan, its organization, and the various factors that have contributed to its present form. One will find here a summary of its story, including the *Bhagavadgītā,* and in non-technical language an elementary account of its mythology, its ethical and moral outlook, and its philosophy. References are given in every chapter to more technical and detailed expositions in the professional literature.

Another part of this book is devoted to an examination of the literary history of the *Mahābhārata.* It was carried eastward by priests and traders of the expanding Hindu colonial empire of the first millennium, to Southeast Asia and the Indonesian archipelago. Also, a brief assessment is made of the *Mahābhārata*'s influence on the West and its status in modern India.

Contents

Chronological Table

1800 B.C.	Composition of the Vedas and their ancillary literature.
1200 B.C.	
c.350 B.C.	A grammarian teaches the formation of the word *Mahābhārata.*
329 B.C.	Alexander the Great leaves India.
c.150 B.C.	Heliodorus leaves an inscription quoting a verse resembling a *Mahābhārata* stanza.
A.D. 28	Vergil composes his *Aeneid.*
c.50	Aśvaghoṣa, a converted Buddhist, shows great familiarity with *Mahābhārata* episodes and thought.
c.400	Kālidāsa bases a play on a *Mahābhārata* episode.
c.550	In the next 1000 years, other Sanskrit writers follow suit.
c.650	A Thai inscription from Veal Kantel names the *Mahābhārata.*
c.700	A Nālandā copperplate inscription from the King of Java mentions five *Mahābhārata* figures.
c.750 ?	The philosopher Śaṃkara writes a commentary on the *Bhagavad-gitā.*
902	Translation into Tamil.
996	Translation into Kannaḍa.
c.1050	Translation into Old Javanese.
1160	Translation into Telugu commenced.
	Benedetto Antelami sculpts an episode originating in the *Mahābhārata,* in a Christian church.
c.1200	Oldest manuscript of the *Mahābhārata.*
c.1200	In Cambodia's Angkor-Wat Temple, scenes from the *Mahābhārata* are sculptured.
c.1250	On Java, the Caṇḍi Jago shows sculptures inspired by a *Mahābhārata* episode.
c.1450	Translation into Orīya.
c.1550	Translations into Assamese, Gujarātī, and Hindī.
1585	Translation into Persian, the *Razm Nāma,* completed.
	The Man-in-the-Well story reaches Japan via Christian missionaries.
c.1650	Translation into Malayālam, Marāṭhī, and Bengalī.
1785	*Bhagavad-gītā* translated into English.
1834	First printed edition of the *Mahābhārata.*
1883-96	Translation into English.
1929-66	Critical Edition.

Condensed Genealogical Table (See p. 48)

Duhṣanta x Śakuntalā

Bharata

Satyavatī x Śantanu x Gaṅgā → Bhīṣma

Vyāsa x Ambikā (x) Vicitravīrya (x) Ambālikā x Vyāsa

Sūrya Dharma   Vāyu Indra   Aśvins

x x Kuntī x x   (x) Pāṇḍu   (x) Mādrī x   Dhṛtarāṣṭra

Karṇa Yudhiṣṭhira   Bhīma Arjuna   Nakula Sahadeva   Duryodhana, etc. and 1 daughter

Abhimanyu

Parikṣit

Janamejaya

CHAPTER 1

Introduction

THE *Mahābhārata,* the great story of the battle between the descendants of Bharata was composed some twenty centuries ago by an anonymous Indian bard, or group of bards, in an unknown place somewhere in northern India. It is not known where or when it was sung first, but in the course of time it spread over thousands upon thousands of villages and towns in India, from the Himalayas in the north all over the Gangetic plain to the far south. Everywhere the people listened and marveled at the miraculous exploits of the mighty Pāṇḍu brothers, the just warriors whose battle against their evil opponents carried within it overtones of the struggle between good and evil which every man and woman experiences in his life. The *Mahābhārata* did not remain confined to India: as the Indian hegemony spread in the middle of the first millennium of our era, the Great Epic followed. To the primitive peoples of Southeast Asia and Indonesia it explained and became identified with the power and magic of the Indian intruders and it soon was incorporated into the cultures of these peoples.

When it spread westward from India, however, it was blocked for a long time by the formidable religious sentiments of the Islamic people who frowned upon the heterodox ethical pronouncements of the Epic. And when the *Mahābhārata* reached the West in the beginning of the nineteenth century, it encountered a culture with its own epics, its own religious literature, and foremost of all, its own critical standards to which a literary work ought to conform in order to be acceptable. The literary world found it difficult to fit the *Mahābhārata* into any one of its already established literary categories. It is neither a purely religious work, nor a genuine epic,[1] nor a romance, nor a philosophical treatise, but contains elements of all these Western literary forms, as well as others. Critics called it a "literary jungle," a "literary monstrosity." [2] Serious students of Indian thought were appalled by the trite plots and obvious moral tendentiousness of some of its stories. On the other hand, the student of world literature despaired of plodding through the *Mahābhārata*'s lengthy speculative passages. As a result, the *Mahābhārata* was fragmentized. Editions appeared of parts of it, such as the *Bhagavad-gītā,* the *Mokṣadharma,* philosophical treatises, and also lighter episodes, such as the *Nala* story, the *Sāvitrī* and occasionally, the *Śakuntalā* story. The epic narrative proper was relegated to books dealing with Indian mythology and so it has become increasingly difficult to gain an appreciation of the *Mahābhārata* in the way it is viewed in India, as a unitary, complete work of art.

This book cannot hope to achieve that end, but will take the position that we are dealing with a foreign work which, though it may not conform to our own standards of great literature, yet is an unerring means for understanding ancient Hindu India and its great tradition. It is a thoroughly Indian work.

The *Mahābhārata* is one of two epics in Indian literature. The other one, the *Rāmāyaṇa,* is much shorter. The *Mahābhārata* is the longest epic in the world. It is encyclopedic in outlook, but its tenuous narrative is epic in character, describing the martial exploits of a number of heroes united in their opposition to the tyranny of a rival group that is bent on destroying them. Around this core are dozens upon dozens of subordinate narratives which at best present the background of the feud and the genealogy of the heroes, and otherwise aim at setting the moral tone against which the narrative moves. At worst, they are pointless narrations of an entertaining or didactic nature.

For India as a whole, the Epic has been very important. If we assume that the genius of a highly cultured group of Brahmans in the first centuries of our era has welded together a mass of the most incredibly dissimilar stories with the aim of establishing a new Hindu tradition in opposition to the prevailing Buddhist doctrines, then we can only marvel at their success. From temple to temple, from court to court, from festival to festival the Epic was carried, until it became part of the unconscious heritage of every Hindu, Jain, and Sikh growing up in India. As such, the importance of the Epic to India is not unlike the significance that Homer and Hesiod together held for Greece: here the Hindu finds his mythology, history, and laws for everyday living and his philosophy. Hindu dramatists drew on the legends of valor, piety and love, transforming them to suit their own interpretations. Religious leaders quoted it to elucidate their views and to emphasize that their assertions were sanctioned by tradition, Hindu tradition.

We may criticize the *Mahābhārata* for many technical deficiencies: its composers never tire of retelling a story, even if the details do not agree in each version, or even if the actions of a hero are quite contrary to the teachings of their masters and even if a character describes the outcome of events in a manner different than the author has just related it. Inconsistency, looseness of arrangement, repetitiveness, distinguish it from such relatively well-arranged and well-composed narratives as the *Knights of the Round Table* or the *Aeneid.* The *Mahābhārata*'s Homer dozed all too often. We shall not refrain from such criticisms, but, on the other hand, should not forget that it perhaps never was the intention of the authors to present a coherent exposition of morality in peace and war. We are probably closer to understanding its underlying theme if we recollect its self-characterization: "That which is found in this work may be found elsewhere, but whatever is not found here, does not occur outside of it," [3] a formidable design but one that accounts for the *Mahābhārata*'s uncommon heterogeneity.

The Epic is related in eighteen books, or *Parvans,* of greatly varying lengths. Each has a name referring to an event in the book. They are in order:

1. *Ādi-parvan* "Origins," containing the genealogies and youthful adventures of the conflicting parties.
2. *Sabhā-parvan* "The Gambling Hall," which relates the fateful gambling match leading to the Pāṇḍava brothers' exile.
3. *Āraṇyaka-parvan* "The Forest," describing the Pāṇḍavas' sojourn as exiles in the forest.
4. *Virāṭa-parvan* "At King Virāṭa's Court."
5. *Udyoga-parvan* "Preparations" (for war).
6. *Bhīṣma-parvan* "Bhīṣma's Generalship," containing the *Bhagavad-gītā.*
7. *Droṇa-parvan* "Droṇa's Generalship"
8. *Karṇa-parvan* "Karṇa's Generalship"
9. *Śalya-parvan* "Śalya's Generalship"
10. *Sauptika-parvan* "The Assault by Night"
11. *Strī-parvan* "The Women"
12. *Śānti-parvan* "Peace"

13. *Anuśāsana-parvan* "Instruction"
14. *Āśvamedhika-parvan* "The Horse-sacrifice"
15. *Āśramavāsika-parvan* "The Sojourn at the Hermitage"
16. *Mausala-parvan* "The Iron Club"
17. *Mahāprasthānika-parvan* "The Great Departure"
18. *Svargārohaṇa-parvan* "The Ascent to Heaven"

An appendix to the *Mahābhārata* is the *Harivaṃśa,* a devotional work celebrating the exploits of Lord Kṛṣṇa. In form and structure it resembles the later Purāṇic works and we shall disregard it.

The word *Mahābhārata-* is a compound of the words *mahā* "large, great" and *bhārata-* "battle of the Bhāratas." The Bhāratas were a tribe of Aryans known from Vedic antiquity who claimed a legendary Bharata as their ancestor.[4] At the time the battle begins they survive in two large clans, the Kurus, or Kauravas, and the Pāṇḍus, or Pāṇḍavas, cousins and deadly enemies. At the time the narrative begins, the battle has long been over and only the Pāṇḍus' offspring survive.

CHAPTER 2

The Epic Story

I *Origins* (Ādi-parvan)

THE *Mahābhārata* begins when the *Sūta* "wandering bard" Ugraśravas, in the presence of a number of wise and illustrious men gathered for a twelve-year sacrifice in honor of King Parikṣit of Hāstinapura, announces that he will recite the *Mahābhārata* in the same way as he had heard it some years before from the sage Vaiśaṃpāyana, who in turn had been taught the story by the worshipful Vyāsa (1.1).[1]

"Having wandered to many sacred watering places and shrines," he continues, "I went to that holy abode called Samantapañcaka which is worshipped by the twice-born castes and in ancient days was the scene of the battle between Pāṇḍavas and Kurus and all other lords of the earth. Anxious to meet you, I have sped thence to your presence." Upon their request, he relates the origin of the world, how it evolved from a Giant Egg which gave rise in turn to all gods, demigods, monsters and men, adding: "Whatever wonderful can be seen here in the world, be it moving or fixed, all that shall be destroyed again at the end of this world, with the dissolution of this Era. And with the commencement of other Eras, just as the characteristics of a season appear in season, in many forms in the course of time, so these appear, exactly alike." Then follows a detailed genealogy of the gods (1.1) and a summary of the contents of the *Mahābhārata,* interspersed with numerous anecdotal stories, the so-called *Parva-saṃgraha* (1.2). He explains the events that led to the performance of Janamejaya's snake sacrifice reaching back far into the mythological past when the snakes had refused to aid their mother Kadrū to win a wager by crooked means, after the churning of the ocean (1.8-31). So they to perish in the flames of Janamejaya's sacrifice. ..urse comes to fruition when the king of snakes kills . father, Parikṣit, treacherously. The son is roused to a ..w of revenge to exterminate all snakes from the surface of ..n by means of a snake sacrifice. In the latter, snakes are lured a large fire by the powerful magical formulas of priests. The ..esign is frustrated through the intervention of gods who save the king of snakes from being roasted (1.9-53).

At this point, the Sūta, by introducing Vyāsa into his narrative, quoting him directly, begins the story all over again, giving a variant version of the genealogy of the gods and the beings that sprang from them. Next, he presents a detailed exposition of the genealogy of the house of Kuru, from whom both the feuding parties, Pāṇḍavas and Kauravas, descend (1.54-61). The mythical ancestor of both was a prince called Bharata and his birth is told in one of the fine episodes of the *Mahābhārata,* the story of Śakuntalā (1.62-69).

The mighty king Duḥṣanta once goes into the forest with a great retinue to hunt for wild animals. After an exhausting chase he becomes separated from his following and wanders into a beautiful hermitage on the bank of the River Mālinī. Upon his summons, not the hermit but his comely adopted daughter Śakuntalā appears. Having offered him hospitality, she explains that her father is not home but will return in an instant. Observing that she is young and beautiful, he has her tell the story of her life and then proceeds to win her favor: "Be my wife, O girl of the lovely hips, tell me what I should do for you. Golden garlands, robes, a pair of ear-rings made of pure gold from various towns, beautiful, with pearls and jewels, O beautiful one, I shall give you now; also golden bracelets and much more and rugs of black antelope fur. Let my whole kingdom be yours now. Become my wife, O lovely one and marry me according to the Gāndharva rite, O timid one, right here, O beautiful one." Śakuntalā is not unwilling but prefers that her father give her away to the king. The latter remonstrates with a long discourse on duty and morality which convinces the innocent hermit girl that the proper thing for her to do is to yield to his demands. Yet, before giving herself to him she insists that any male issue that may come from their union, should become the heir to Duḥṣanta's throne. Without giving it a thought the king agrees. He has his way with her and departs, promising to have her taken to his capital later. But he never calls on her, and in time a son is born; he is a sturdy six-year-old before she decides to go to the king's capital, Hāstinapura, to present him to his father.

Once in the king's residence, the simple hermit girl calls on the king with their son. Having made her obeisance, she speaks: "Here is your son, O king; let him be anointed as your heir apparent. For by you, O king, this boy who looks like a god, was begotten upon me. Now act according to your promise, O best of men: remember the promise as you made it earlier at our union in the hermitage of Kaṇva, O you of great fortune!" But to Śakuntalā's great astonishment, the king rebuffs her rudely, calling her a nasty name and declaring that he does not remember anything: she may go, if she likes, or stay, but he is not concerned. Driven to despair, then indignation, Śakuntalā, looking him straight in the face bursts forth in an impassioned speech, one of the finest in the epic: "Although you know the truth very well, O king, why do you talk in this manner (saying) like any commoner: 'I do not know'? In this matter, I know, it is your heart that is witness to its truth or falsehood; alas, Sire, do not degrade yourself. He who being one thing, behaves differently, what evil would he not commit, being like a thief robbing himself? Do not despise me for having come on my own accord, as I am devoted to my husband. I am worthy of respect and you do not treat me courteously, your own wife, who has come to you. . . . She is a true wife who is skillful in the home; she is a true wife who bears children. She is a true wife whose husband is as dear to her as her life; she is a true wife who is devoted to her husband. A wife is half the man, the wife is the best friend; the wife is the root of the threefold morality; Righteousness, Wealth and Pleasure; the wife is the friend for one who is about to die; with their wives men can perform sacrifices, with wives they can perform domestic rites. Men with wives are happy, men with wives are full of good fortune. Friends in solitude are these sweet-speeched women. They are fathers on the occasion of religious acts and mothers to the woe-begone. Even in the wilderness, to the traveller his wife brings security; he who has a wife is trusted by everyone, therefore, a wife is the best goal. Also, when the husband dies and passes on to the asperities (of the hereafter), falling all alone, his wife who is ever devoted to him follows. Should the wife die first then she waits, having died for her husband; if the husband dies first, she follows after him. For this reason, O king, is marriage needful that a husband obtain a wife in this world and hereafter. The wise say that a man by himself causes himself to be born as his son; therefore, a man should look at her who is the mother of his baby boy, as his own mother. A father looking at the face of a son born to his wife, as if it were his own in a mirror, experiences joy like a pious man who has attained heaven. Men burning with mental grief, or afflicted by disease experience joy in their wives, like a person tormented by heat, in water. Even if very angry at charming women, a wise man will not say an unkind thing, having considered that pleasure, love, and morality are all dependent on them. A lovely woman is ever the sacred field of one's own birth: were even sages able to procreate without a wife? What greater happiness is there for a father when he embraces his son who has come running up to him, covered with dirt from the earth? Why then do you despise scornfully your son who has come to you on his own accord and is looking at you with eager anticipation?" (68.15-53).

Duhṣanta is hardly moved by Śakuntalā's plea. "Women usually tell lies," he says, "Why should I believe you? You look like a trollop to me, so you may go where you like." But Śakuntalā does not give up and continues to plead until a heavenly voice announces to the king that he should accept his son. Then he relents, picks up his boy and caresses him. To Śakuntalā he explains that he had to act as he did, because without some divine authorization, his subjects would never have accepted the boy as the heir-apparent. The boy is named Bharata "fire," and the heroes of the Mahābhārata trace their lineage back to him.

The Śakuntalā episode is only one of many mythical stories that tradition associates with the ancestors of the Kuru race. Another famous one is that of King Yayāti who ruled over a large part of northern India. He was cursed to become old immediately unless he succeeded in finding a young person who would assume the burden of his old age in exchange for his youth. In vain, Yayāti begged his four sons, but only the youngest one, Pūru, sacrificed his youth and allowed his father to enjoy many more years of pleasurable living. In time, Yayāti restored Pūru's youth and appointed him successor to the throne (1.71-88).

The ancestry of the Pāṇḍavas and Kurus which forms the subject of the next few chapters, is complex. The Pāṇḍavas' eponymous ancestor, Pāṇḍu, was a powerful king of Hāstinapura whose older brother, Dhṛtarāṣṭra, had been unable to become king on account of his blindness. Dhṛtarāṣṭra begat one hundred sons and a daughter of his wife, virtuous Gāndhārī. They are the wicked Kurus who will combat their brothers, the Pāṇḍavas. Pāṇḍu himself had two wives, Kuntī and Mādrī but was unable to beget children. After a victorious reign he repaired to the mountains to pray for offspring and in response the gods granted him five children. By the God of Justice, Dharma,

Kuntī conceived Yudhiṣṭhira, by the God of the wind Bhīma, and by Indra, Arjuna. His other wife, Mādrī, was blessed with the twins Nakula and Sahadeva by the celestial twin gods, the Aśvins. Soon afterward Pāṇḍu died as the result of attempting intercourse in defiance of a curse. He was cremated and his one wife Mādrī ascended the pyre voluntarily. Kuntī took the five princes to the capital city of Hāstinapura to be raised at the court of their uncle Dhṛtarāṣṭra, together with their one hundred cousins (1.89-118).

Soon it appears that the Pāṇḍu brothers excel their cousins in all games of strength and skill. Bhīma especially by his impetuosity and physical power often injures his cousins who begin to hate him so much that the eldest, Duryodhana, plots in many ways to destroy him by ruses and ambushes. But Bhīma's phenomenal strength carries him through these trials triumphantly (1.119).

Two prominent educators of the time are appointed as the princes' tutors. One is Bhīṣma, son of the River Ganges, an oldtime friend and counselor of Dhṛtarāṣṭra and Pāṇḍu. Bhīṣma is a warrior by caste, but had early taken a vow of celibacy to which he adheres rigidly. He is portrayed as a man of great wisdom and spiritual insight and as a propounder and follower of all that is righteous. He teaches the princes the warrior code and the strategy of battle. The other tutor is Droṇa, also a warrior, who has undertaken the princes' education for political ends, as will appear soon (see p. 10). He trains the princes in all the sciences of warfare, such as mace fighting, chariot combat, and archery (1.120-22). After some time, Arjuna believes himself to be the best archer in the country. Then he discovers to his dismay that a despicable Niṣāda boy,[2] Ekalavya, who worships Droṇa from a distance, has practiced shooting arrows at a clay image so effectively that Arjuna fears to be inferior to him. After he has complained to Droṇa the latter goes to the Niṣāda boy and forces him to cut off his right thumb. Arjuna becomes happy again.

Duryodhana and Bhīma are equals in mace fighting, Yudhiṣṭhira is the best chariot fighter, Nakula and Sahadeva excel in sword fighting, but Arjuna, besides being the most accomplished archer, surpasses the others in every weapon. Another powerful warrior is Droṇa's own son, Aśvatthāman, who receives his instruction together with the princes (1.123).

At their final contest in weapon skill the whole palace is present in the arena to witness the games. Droṇa enters dressed in white and supervises the proceedings: riding, sword-fighting, archery. Duryodhana and Bhīma hold a mace contest which remains undecided: then Arjuna gives a demonstration of archery which leaves the audience breathless. But just before it is over, the gate to the arena is opened with a great tumult and a splendidly attired warrior, Karṇa strides in. He is the illegitimate son of Kuntī, Arjuna's mother, by the Sungod, but has been raised by a coachman of low social rank, so that no one suspects his divine birth. The Pāṇḍavas know him only by sight. He proudly announces that he will match and outdo Arjuna's weapon feats and does so with Droṇa's permission, much to Duryodhana's satisfaction. But Arjuna coldly challenges him to a duel. Both shoot arrows at one another until one of the spectators, Kṛpa, raises a point of order: he demands that both warriors identify themselves, giving their names and royal lineage before continuing the combat. Pale with anger and afraid of derision, the coacher's son remains silent, but at this point Duryodhana nobly intercedes and appoints Karṇa king of the Añgas. This status gives him a title and an opportunity to continue the battle. This event is significant, for from that day on until he expires on the battlefield, Karṇa aligns himself with the Kurus and remains loyal and faithful to them even after he learns that the Pāṇḍus are his half-brothers. But Bhīma scornfully mocks Karṇa suggesting he take a whip rather than a bow to fight Arjuna. Before the quarrel becomes critical, the sun sets and the contenders go home (1.124-27).

When the princes have ended their apprenticeship with Droṇa he asks them for the preceptor's fee to which he is entitled. He demands that the princes assist him in the overthrow of Drupada, a neighboring king with whom he is having a feud. They comply and defeat Drupada whereupon Droṇa seizes half of his kingdom (128).

Soon afterwards, the sons of Dhṛtarāṣṭra, jealous of Yudhiṣṭhira's popularity with the people of Kuru country, seek a means of disposing of their cousins. With the cognizance of their weak father they send the Pāṇḍava brothers and their mother to a distant part of the country to reside in a house plastered with lac, a kind of gum. One of their collaborators is instructed to set fire to the house when the opportunity arises, but Yudhiṣṭhira hears of it in time. To elude their persecutors, they set fire to the house themselves one night, after having invited five Niṣāda boys and their mother to spend the night as their guests. By an underground passage they escape from the blaze, and when the citizens find the charred bodies they mistake them for the remains of the Pāṇḍavas. Our heroes, meanwhile, secretly course through the jungle, often carried on Bhīma's powerful back and experience many frightful adventures. As the result of one of these, Bhīma has a brief affair with a Rākṣasa woman whose brother he has killed. From their union springs a monstrous son, half demon and half man, named Ghaṭotkaca (1.129-53).

Drupada, meanwhile, is unable to forget the humiliation he has undergone at the hands of Droṇa. Plotting his revenge, he undergoes severe austerities in order to obtain from a sacrificial fire a son Dhṛṣṭadyumna and a beautiful daughter, Kṛṣṇā, more commonly known as Draupadī, the future wife of the Pāṇḍu brothers. Her fragrance can be smelt a league away. The son is destined to slay Droṇa one day (1.154). In time, Drupada holds a *svayaṃvara* "marriage ceremony by self-choice" [3] for his daughter to which kings from all over the country are invited to compete for her hand, including the Pāṇḍava brothers. Still concerned about being recognized by the Kurus, they vie for Draupadī's hand in the guise of Brahmans. The contest, for which the girl is the prize, consists of bending and stringing a bow and striking a target with five arrows. One after the other, the mighty kings of the earth attempt the feat, only to turn back unsuccessfully, until Arjuna, a strange looking Brahman, indeed, with a towering physique and bulging muscles, strides forward, effortlessly strings the bow and shoots down the target. Accepted by Draupadī he takes her to their temporary dwelling in a potter's shed, where their mother is cooking the food. When Arjuna comes in with his brothers and wife, he jokingly refers to Draupadī as their *bhikṣā* "alms" of the day. Without looking up their mother mumbles: "I hope you will enjoy it together." As a mother's words are sacred, the Pāṇḍavas dare not oppose her and decide on a joint marriage with Draupadī. To her father, Drupada, they reveal their identity and after some persuasion he agrees to the outlandish match. They become allies (174-90).

At the *svayaṃvara* their first meeting with Kṛṣṇa has taken place. He is a king of the Yādavas who is to play an important role in their lives. He immediately seeks their friendship and sends costly gifts to their wedding (191).

As the news of their wedding spreads, the Kurus discover that their cousins are still alive. Dhṛtarāṣṭra, who had experienced pangs of remorse at their supposed death in the gum house, is visibly relieved, to the great annoyance of his sons. At Bhīṣma's advice, they decide to offer the Pāṇḍavas half the kingdom, the eastern half, in the region called Khāṇḍava-prastha. The Pāṇḍavas accept the proposal and move to their new domain where they erect a beautiful city, Indraprastha. Then Arjuna goes away for twelve years on a journey of adventures to the north and south. In the southern town of Maṇalūra he marries a princess and stays with her for three years. Thereupon he visits Kṛṣṇa on the west coast and makes off with his sister Subhadrā. At the end of twelve years he returns to Indraprastha with his new wife. She bears him a son, Abhimanyu, and Draupadī also bears each of the brothers a son (192-213).

One day Agni, the god of fire, instructs Arjuna and Kṛṣṇa to aid him in destroying the Khāṇḍava forest. He stipulates that no creatures may escape alive from the forest and presents Arjuna with a magic bow and two inexhaustible quivers, and Kṛṣṇa with a never failing disk and mace. Agni attacks the forest, consuming it in a terrible holocaust, while Arjuna and Kṛṣṇa, stationed at one end, shoot down every creature that tries to save itself. Only an *Asura* "demon," Maya by name, who had been held captive by the king of snakes, is spared. As an additional reward for the great achievement, Arjuna asks Indra for magic weapons, but is told that he will receive them as soon as Śiva thinks he is worthy of them (1.214-22).

Here ends the first book.

II *The Gambling Hall* (Sabhā-parvan)

After the burning of the forest, the Asura Maya shows his gratitude by building a magnificent palace for Yudhiṣṭhira in Indraprastha. Arjuna personally receives from him a conch shell named Devadatta and Bhīma gets a mace. By Maya's magic the palace is built in a short time, and its official opening is attended by thousands of gods, demigods, and people. Among the invited guests is the celebrated sage Nārada, an immortal wanderer who conveys messages from the gods to people and assists everyone with his sage advice (2.1-6). To entertain the guests he describes five heavens belonging to the five deities, Indra, Yama, Varuṇa, Kubera, and Brahma. Indra's heaven, the ultimate destination of all valiant warriors, is portrayed in part as follows:

Nārada said: "For one thing, Indra's celestial palace is shining, made as it is with acts of sacrifice. It was built by Indra himself, O scion of Kuru's race (Yudhiṣṭhira), with a splendor equal to that of the sun. Air-borne and capable of going anywhere, it exends one hundred *yojanas* in width, 150 in length and is five *yojanas* high.[4] It is free of old age, sorrow, fatigue, disease, and is pleasant, beautiful, furnished with rooms and seats, enjoyable, embellished with heavenly trees. In that palace, O Pārtha (Yudhiṣṭhira), on a magnificent throne, sits the Lord of Gods with Śacī, the great lord's wife, who is Śrī 'majesty' and Lakṣmī 'good fortune,' O Bhārata. Possessing an indescribable beauty, with a diadem and red bracelets around his arms, in spotless garments, wearing colorful garlands, he sits with modesty, fame and majesty. In that hall, Maruts on all sides, O king, and all (others) who are the object of domestic rites, attend upon the great-souled Lord of one hundred sacrifices, all the time: the Siddhas and the Royal Sages, the Sādhyas and the hosts of gods. All these with their retinues, divinely beautiful, well-embellished, attend upon the illustrious king of the gods, the crusher of enemies. Thus all the divine sages, O Pārtha, attend upon Indra, the spotless ones who have shaken off their sins and glow like fires, full of splendor, partaking of Soma, free from sin, their fatigue disappeared. . . Others present are the waters and plants, Faith, Intelligence, Material Wealth, Righteousness and Pleasure and also the Lightning, O Pāṇḍava. And waterbearing clouds, winds, thunder, the eastern point of compass, twenty-seven fires bearing up oblations, Agni-Soma and Indra-Agni, Mitra, Savitṛ and Aryaman. . . , the sacrificial oblations and gifts to Brahmans, spoonfuls (of Soma) and laudations everywhere and the formels that bring oblation, . . . all these are there together. So too celestial nymphs, O king, enrapturing musicians with various dances, recitations and songs and with laughter make the King of the Gods happy, O lord, the master of one hundred sacrifices, extolling with praises as well as auspicious formulas and acts of sacrifice and heroism the illustrious slayer of Bala and Vṛtra. All classes of sages adorned with wreaths, decorated, are coming and going in various celestial vehicles which blaze like fires. . . These and many others, self-restrained, under strict vows, come in cars blazing like the moon, looking beautiful like Soma, at Brahman's orders, O king, Bhṛgu and the seven sages. I have seen this palace, O king, called Puṣkaramālinī" (2.7).

Nārada goes on to describe the divine abodes of the other four gods, displaying a tedious lack of imagination. The pleasures in each of them resemble very much those in Indra's heaven. He concludes by conveying a message from Pāṇḍu who is in Brahma's heaven, to Yudhiṣṭhira that he should undertake a sacrifice of royal consecration. After some reflection, Yudhiṣṭhira agrees (2.8-11).

Yudhiṣṭhira invites Kṛṣṇa to Indraprastha to ask him for advice about the sacrifice. He will have to conquer the whole world, Kṛṣṇa says, before he may undertake it. Kṛṣṇa believes that the only obstacle to Yudhiṣṭhira's conquest is King Jarāsaṃdha of Māgadha who is in the process of subduing other countries, taking their kings with him as captives. He has brought together eighty-six of them in the mountain

Girivraja and has vowed to sacrifice them all to Mahādeva as soon as he has imprisoned one hundred. Among the captured are some of Kṛṣṇa's clansmen. "Defeat that king, O Yudhiṣṭhira," adds Kṛṣṇa, "and you will surely become universal monarch." Yudhiṣṭhira hesitates to risk his brothers' lives on the campaign, but Arjuna brushes aside his objections: "We have the arms, the energy and the ability to fight; I like nothing better than violence. It is our duty to perform acts of heroism, born as we are in a noble line of warriors!" (2.12-16).

Arjuna, Bhīma and Kṛṣṇa agree to go, not as an army opposing Jarāsaṃdha's might, but in disguise to defeat him stealthily, "like a stream uprooting a tree." At Kṛṣṇa's suggestion they disguise themselves as Brahman students in yellow robes and set out forMāgadha, an opulent city made rich by Jarāsaṃdha's conquests. Near the gate is a beautiful shrine, the delight of the citizens of Māgadha, but the heroes pierce it with their arrows. They enter the city and laughingly snatch garlands from the florists in the market place and also steal rings and clothes. Then they head for the palace to be received personally by Jarāsaṃdha, who pays this honor to all Brahmans who visit him. But the guests decline his hospitality and soon Jarāsaṃdha becomes suspicious: "How is it," he asks, "that you pretend to be Brahman students, yet deck yourselves with colorful robes and paste and have all the marks of a warrior?" Kṛṣṇa piously replies that they are *Kṣatriyas* of a special type, who have undertaken a vow of the Brahman caste to gain wealth and property. Their vow prevents them from accepting hospitality from an enemy. Astonished, Jarāsaṃdha states that he is unaware of ever having done them any harm. Then Kṛṣṇa reveals their true purpose: they have come to the rescue of the captured kings whose intended massacre is a violation of the warrior code. Either they are released immediately, or Jarāsaṃdha will have to fight a duel with one of his guests. Jarāsaṃdha replies that he has never acted against the warrior code, for every king had been defeated before he was captured. Once a king is defeated his life is in the hands of his captor, so Kṛṣṇa's charge is unfounded. Even so, he is prepared to decide the issue with a duel (2.18-19).

Before the combat Jarāsaṃdha consecrates his son to succeed him in case he loses. Then "taking off his diadem and binding up his hair, he stood before Bhīma like an ocean overflowing its shores. 'I will fight you,' he said. Then they began to wrestle and fought terribly, those two heroes of great strength, like tigers in human form. Lunging at each other with their long arms, hammering blows at each others' broad shoulders with their fists which were like maces of iron, striking with their knee-joints, they mangled one another dreadfully, all the while hurling bitter insults." For fourteen days the terrible encounter lasted, then Kṛṣṇa saw signs of fatigue in Jarāsaṃdha. He spoke: "Do not apply too much force, O Bhīma, or your opponent may die too soon!" Then Bhīma resolved to end the battle. Lifting Jarāsaṃdha high above his head, he whirled him around a full one hundred times, then brought him down with force and snapped his back on his own knee. Jarāsaṃdha died with a horrible cry, which was drowned in Bhīma's roar of victory.

Kṛṣṇa quickly commandeered Jarāsaṃdha's chariot and with the brothers went out to liberate the king's captives in Mount Girivraja. In gratitude they offered him jewels and treasures. Then all departed for their respectives countries (2.20-22).

Next the Pāṇḍava brothers set out to conquer the world for Yudhiṣṭhira. After lengthy campaigns which take Arjuna to the North, Bhīma to the East, Sahadeva to the South and Nakula to the West, and mighty battles with barbarian kings from which they emerge victorious, the brothers return to Indraprastha. Many geographical names are listed in regions inside and outside India (2.23-29). Kṛṣṇa appears again and suggests the royal sacrifice be commenced. Thousands of kings, chieftains and headmen come to pay their tribute to the new ruler of the world and are lavishly entertained in the magnificent new palace (2.33-42). At the concluding ceremony of the consecration of Yudhiṣṭhira as supreme world monarch, gifts of honor are to be distributed to the guests. At Bhīṣma's suggestion the honor of receiving the first prize should go to Kṛṣṇa. But King Śiśupāla of the Cedis objects: in contemptuous tones he belittles Kṛṣṇa's achievements and holds him responsible for the murder of Jarāsaṃdha. Yudhiṣṭhira's conciliatory efforts are fruitless. A dispute breaks out between Śiśupāla and Kṛṣṇa with recriminations that point to a longstanding feud between the two. Finally, Kṛṣṇa produces his discus and unexpectedly severs Śiśupāla's head, in the midst of the assembly. All behold how Śiśupāla's life-energy moves out of his body and is absorbed by Kṛṣṇa (2.23-42).

Upon the conclusion of the sacrifice, Duryodhana and his maternal uncle, Śakuni, remain behind to inspect the palace. They meet with all sorts of comical mishaps. Duryodhana mistakes a crystal floor for a pond and, lifting up his clothes, attempts to wade through it. Some time later he falls into a pond believing it made of crystal, to the great hilarity of Bhīma and the palace staff. Humiliated and consumed with envy of the Pāṇḍavas' prosperity, Duryodhana returns to Hāstinapura declaring that life holds no attraction for him any more. Either he will have to bring the Pāṇḍu brothers to ruin or he shall take his own life. Śakuni consoles him and suggests that there is a way in which the Pāṇḍu brothers may be destroyed. Duryodhana readily agrees with a plan to invite the brothers for a game of dice with their respective kingdoms as stakes. Śakuni is the best dice player in the world, so the risks are small. The old king, Dhṛtarāṣṭra, will not agree until it has been pointed out that he himself will benefit from the victory also (2.43-51).

The old Vidura, a friend of the Pāṇḍavas, is dispatched to Indraprastha to challenge them to a game of dice, much against his will. Yudhiṣṭhira believes it is against his moral code to decline a challenge and so the brothers, with Draupadī, set out for Hāstinapura where they are entertained by songs of beautiful damsels before going to sleep. The next day they assemble in the magnificent gambling hall, especially erected for this occasion. Yudhiṣṭhira will play for the Pāṇḍus and Śakuni for the Kuru family. Yudhiṣṭhira declares that he considers gambling a crafty and cunning game in which the more deceitful will gain the victory, but Śakuni counters his arguments with a smile: "Just as a skilled warrior will defeat a less experienced one, so the strongest gambler will win. What is immoral about that? Of course, if you wish to quit you may do so . . ." (2.52-53).

So the game begins with all the kings of the realm standing by as spectators.[5] They name their stakes and play thirteen games, all of which are won by Śakuni. Yudhiṣṭhira, meanwhile, has lost all his personal possessions, his slaves, his subjects and his country. All that remains to him are his four brothers, his own person, and Draupadī. Intoxicated by the gambling spirit he stakes the twins, Bhīma and Arjuna and loses them all. Then he stakes his own person and loses again, while his brothers, reduced to slaves, sit nearby in stony silence. Only one more stake remains, their wife Draupadī. With the words: "I shall play with you, staking Draupadī who is neither tall nor short, neither plump nor thin, a maiden with blue curly locks whose face looks like the lotus or the jasmine, of red lips and a slender waist," he stakes her. The kings are aghast and censure Yudhiṣṭhira, but Śakuni excitedly plays and wins again. Duryodhana, still filled with envy and bitterness, eager to humiliate the Pāṇḍu brothers, orders Draupadī to be hauled before the assembly to sweep the floors as befits a slave girl.

Vidura objects loudly but nobody pays attention to him. Draupadī is soon dragged in by her hair by Duryodhana's brother, Duḥśāsana. Crying dismally she is ridiculed by the Kurus while the Pāṇḍavas sit with bowed heads, unable to look at the shameful treatment meted out to their wife. Then a legal point arises: Vidura argues that Yudhiṣṭhira could not have lost Draupadī as a stake, because at the time he had lost his own freedom already. Her husbands may be slaves, but she is still free. Yudhiṣṭhira himself is asked to arbitrate this point, but remains silent. Bhīma angrily threatens to burn his hands to make him speak up, but Arjuna calms him. Then their enemy Karṇa, by playing up the immoral relationship between the Pāṇḍavas and their common wife, convinces the audience that Draupadī has truly become a slave. It would even be proper to strip all of them of their clothes. The Pāṇḍu brothers silently take off their garments and Duḥśāsana begins to rip off Draupadī's clothes. But miraculously, a new garment appears for every one that is removed, until Duḥśāsana sits down exhausted. Bhīma swears that one day he will rip open Duḥśāsana's breast and drink his blood. With the approval of all spectators, Duryodhana calls on Draupadī to let her husbands decide whether she had become his slave woman or not, but Yudhiṣṭhira persists in his silence and the other brothers may not speak before their senior. To insult them even more, Duryodhana bares his left thigh to Draupadī. Raging with fury Bhīma pronounces the terrible oath that he will not go to the region of his ancestors, before he had broken that thigh bone (2.54-63).

Dhṛtarāṣṭra, who cannot tolerate witnessing the humiliation of his kinsmen any longer, reproves Duryodhana and grants Draupadī her own freedom and that of her husbands. But no sooner have the Pāṇḍus walked out of the assembly, bitter and silent, than Duryodhana and Śakuni panic the irresolute king into believing that the Pāṇḍus are about to return for a bloody war of vengeance. In spite of Gāndhārī's earnest pleas, he consents to have the Pāṇḍus called back for a second, decisive game of dice. When they are back, the following agreement is reached: the party that loses the dice game will voluntarily go into exile for twelve years, to live in the forest. During the thirteenth year they will return to society and live among the people for a full year, keeping their identity an absolute secret. If they succeed in concealing their identity for a year, they will regain their kingdom. Should they be recognized, however, then they would have to return to the forest for another twelve years (2.63-67).

The dice are cast and the fateful game is over soon. Yudhiṣṭhira has lost again. Sadly, the brothers prepare to leave for the forest, accompanied by the ridicule and contemptuous words and gestures of the Kurus. Bhīma threatens again that he will drink Duḥśāsana's blood on the battlefield and Arjuna swears he will slay Karṇa. Sahadeva vows he will kill Śakuni and Nakula that he will clear the earth of the remaining sons of Dhṛtarāṣṭra. Yudhiṣṭhira, however, quietly takes leave of all the kings, including Dhṛtarāṣṭra and Vidura blesses him solemnly: "O scion of the Bhārata race, may you derive gentleness from yourself, your life's maintenance from the water, patience from the earth and all splendor from the disk of the sun. Know you that strength comes from the wind and from the creatures the origin of oneself." Kuntī, their mother, remains behind but Draupadī follows her husbands into exile. Clad in deerskins, they form a sorry procession as they file away from the capital. Evil omens accompany their departure while King Dhṛtarāṣṭra, steeped in sorrow, meditates with his charioteer Saṃjaya on the calamity that has befallen his race: "Fate does not come with an upraised club to smash one over the head," muses Saṃjaya. "Its peculiarity is that it makes a man see goodness in evil and evil in goodness" (1.67-72).

III *The Forest* (Āraṇyaka-parvan)

Concerned about not being able to feed all the Brahmans in his retinue, Yudhiṣṭhira's priest recites the Sungod's one hundred and eight names, until the latter appears in person and promises Yudhiṣṭhira an inexhaustible supply of food. They travel north to the Kāmyaka forest where Bhīma slays a giant Rākṣasa. Some time later Vidura visits them there. He had been banished from the court for his open defense of the Pāṇḍavas. Soon Dhṛtarāṣṭra repents and has Vidura come back (3.1-7).

While residing in the forest, the Pāṇḍavas receive numerous guests. Among the first are Kṛṣṇa and his clan members. He apologizes for having been absent from the gambling party, but at the time he was fighting a battle in defence of his capital, Dvārakā, against Salva, the ruler of a flying city. He assures Yudhiṣṭhira that he would have killed Duryodhana, had he only been at the dice game. After his departure the Pāṇḍavas move further west to the Dvaita forest where they camp by a lake (3.8-17). In a fit of depression, Draupadī urges Yudhiṣṭhira to take up arms and fight for his kingdom, complaining bitterly about the insults she has undergone at the hands of the Kurus. Bhīma supports her, accusing Yudhiṣṭhira of weakness and carelessness during the gambling episode. But Yudhiṣṭhira remains firm in his resolve that he cannot go back on his word. He has undertaken to stay in the forest and "a man of honor will sooner die than usurp power by criminal means." Unconvinced, Bhīma pleads to stay thirteen months instead of thirteen years and afterward atone for the sin of breach of word, but Yudhiṣṭhira remains unmoved (3.28-37).

Another visitor is the sage Vyāsa who advises them to return to the Kāmyaka forest, because the wildlife in the Dvaita forest was being depleted (3.37).

Next Arjuna departs to try and obtain a vision of Śiva who will give him divine weapons should he prove himself worthy (see 1.222). He goes to the Himālayas where he practices severe penance by starving himself while standing in an uncomfortable position: With his arms raised and, standing on the tips of his toes he reduces his diet until he finally lives on air only, bathing frequently. The heat of his penance makes the inhabitants of heaven uneasy and they ask Śiva to interfere. The latter assumes the guise of a Kirāta, a wild man of the mountains hunting with bow and arrow. While wrapt in austerities, Arjuna suddenly sees a huge boar, actually a demon in disguise, rushing at him. Warning him with the words: "I have not come here to slay you, but as you attack me, I shall send you to the abode of Yama" (thus clearing himself of the sin of violence), Arjuna picks up his bow and is ready to shoot, when Śiva appears and stops him with the words: "This boar is my quarry, leave it alone." Arjuna ignores him and shoots the boar at the same time the Kirāta lets go of an arrow. The boar is struck by both simultaneously. Arjuna haughtily informs the Kirāta that he has acted against the codes of hunting by interfering with his kill and so has forfeited his life. The wild mountaineer smilingly explains that it was his boar and that he killed it legitimately. "Stay and fight, O wretch!" he concludes. In the bitter combat that ensues Arjuna's weapons prove futile, so he engages his opponent in hand-to-hand combat from which he emerges bruised, mangled, and senseless, Śiva proving the stronger. The latter then reveals himself in all his glory with his trident and consort Umā at his side. Pleased, he presents Arjuna with the Pāśupata weapon to which other gods add other unopposable weapons (3.38-42). Arjuna next has a sojourn in Indra's heaven for five years where he learns to use the divine weapons and receives instruction from a Gandharva (3.43-46).

Meanwhile, the other Pāṇḍavas live in the forest subsisting from the chase and the gathering of fruit. They are concerned about Arjuna's long absence and even the arrival of the sage Lomaśa, dispatched by Indra to report on Arjuna's whereabouts, does not relieve their anxiety. Many holy men pass by to pay their respects and narrate beautiful stories about the instability of man's fate and the unhappiness of other people. Among others, they hear the story of King Nala who fell prey to his passion for dice and deserted his beautiful wife Damayantī (3.50-78).

Nala was a virtuous king of the Niṣadha people. Damayantī a princess of Vidarbha, the most beautiful girl in the world. Without ever having set eyes on one another, they fell in love when they heard about each other's excellent qualities. Once, Nala caught a magic goose in his park whom he used to announce his love to Damayantī. As the latter pined away from unrequited love, her father organized a *svayaṃvara* for her to which four gods, Indra, Agni, Varuṇa, and Yama also decided to go. On their way they met Nala whom they instructed to inform Damayantī that she was to choose one of them. He complied and magically gained admission to Damayantī's quarters where he announced that he was the gods' messenger. But Damayantī replied that she would choose him alone. At the marriage ceremony, however, the gods assumed shapes identical with Nala's. Unable to identify her love, she made an appeal to the gods: "As surely as I am not unfaithful just with word and mind, because of that truth let the gods point out to me just him alone."

Moved by her plea, the gods granted her wish and gave Nala four gifts: the power to have water, to have fire and to cook wherever he wished, and also the ability to walk upright wherever he went, so that he never needed to stoop. Thereupon, his wedding with Damayantī took place. The gods, upon their return to heaven, met two gods of unlucky gambling, Kali and Dvāpara, who had also planned to woo Damayantī. When they heard that Nala had been chosen already, Kali swore that he would destroy Nala.

For a long time, Nala's virtuous behavior prevented Kali from infecting him, but through a slight negligence in the performance of a ritual, Nala finally exposed himself and Kali took possession of the king. Intoxicated with gambling fever, Nala lost all his worldly goods and his kingdom to his brother Puṣkara. With Damayantī he left the city and soon after, while she was asleep he deserted her. When she awakened Damayantī lamented and went out to look for her husband.

A python caught her and would have strangled her but for the intervention of a hunter. Her beauty excited the hunter's desire but when he attempted to force her she cursed him whereupon he fell lifeless to the ground. In a delirious frenzy Damayantī roamed over the countryside looking for her husband. She joined a caravan which subsequently was trampled by a herd of elephants, though she was left unscathed. In Cedi, after being set upon by city men, she was taken into service by the queen as a companion to the princess. Later she returned to her parents in Vidarbha.

Nala, meanwhile, wandered around dispiritedly. He came upon a burning forest, and hearing cries for help he rescued the king of snakes and was rewarded for his efforts by being bitten. The snake's poison deformed Nala, so that he was unrecognizable, but at the same time it tormented the evil god Kali who was still within his system. Nala thereupon hired himself out as groom to the king of Ayodhyā where he was finally tentatively recognized by investigators from Damayantī's court. To learn the truth, Damayantī invited the king and his charioteer to her court. On their way, Nala rid himself of Kali by learning from the king how to guess the number of fruit on a Vibhītaka tree. In return he taught him the science of horse care. At first Damayantī failed to recognize her husband in the deformed Nala, but her servant observed certain miraculous deeds he could perform which corresponded to the gifts Nala had obtained through the grace of the gods at the wedding ceremony. Certain of him now, Damayantī swore by the God Vāyu that she had not been unfaithful, whereupon Nala deigned to take her back, assuming his old form. By gambling, applying the skill he had acquired from the king of Ayodhyā, he regained his kingdom where Damayantī joined him.

The Pāṇḍavas then start on a long pilgrimage visiting holy places all over Central India. They listen to the old tales connected with each place of pilgrimage, such as the story of the demon Ilvala who repeatedly changed his brother into a goat, then killed him and offered him to a Brahman to eat, who died when he revived the goat (3.94). Also they hear the tale of the demons who fled into the sea when Indra killed the demon Vṛtra and made forages from there to kill Brahmans (3.98-101). The sage Agastya, however, drank up the sea, giving the gods an opportunity to slay the demons. The problem of how to refill the ocean was solved after a long time when King Bhagīratha practiced austerities to force god Śiva to come to earth and receive on his head the celestial Ganges. It flowed in a mighty torrent from heaven via Śiva's locks into the ocean bed (3.103-8). They also hear the strange story of the horned hermit boy Ṛśyaśṛṅga who had never seen a girl. One year a devastating drought came over Aṅga country and the king was told that only the presence of Ṛśyaśṛṅga would bring relief. A beautiful courtesan was dispatched to fetch him and after an amusing meeting she seduced him into coming with her, whereupon the rains started (3.110-13). At yet another place, the Pāṇḍavas hear the ancient story of Rāma,[6] son of Jamadagni, the only one among his brothers who was prepared to kill his mother because his father suspected her of impurity. Later, to avenge the death of his father, Rāma wiped out the Kṣatriyas from the earth, filling five lakes with their blood, but he atoned for his violence by giving presents to Brahmans. The Pāṇḍavas visit him at the Mahendra mountain, where he has retired (3.116-17).

At another holy place, near the Narmadā River, Lomaśa relates the story of Cyavana, an austere saint who practiced penance for such a long time that an anthill grew up around him. One day the king came by with his beautiful daughter Sukanyā. Seeting the anthill and the curiously sparkling eyes in the middle, she poked at them playfully with a thorn, unaware of what they were. Cyavanā became so enraged that he cursed the king's whole army with constipation from which he did not relieve them until he had obtained the girl as his wife. He later regained his youth (3.122-24). They hear also of Māndhātṛ's strange birth from his father's side (3.126) and about King Somaka (3.127-28) who sacrificed his son to obtain more offspring. There is also the moving story of King Uśīnara who sacrificed his own flesh by cutting off pieces from his thigh, to compensate a falcon for the loss of his prey, a pigeon which had taken refuge with the king (3.130-31). The sage Bāladhi by severe austerities begat a son who would live as long as the mountains would stand. Conscious of his invulnerability, the son haughtily stalked the earth defying laws and perpetrating mischief. But once he insulted a mighty *ṛṣi* "sage." In revenge the *ṛṣi* had the mountains destroyed by buffaloes whereupon the sinner turned to ashes (3.136).

After many other adventures, the Pāṇḍavas in their fifth year of exile go to the Gandhamādana mountain to await Arjuna. He arrives in Indra's chariot and after giving them a vivid description of what had happened to him (3.155-73), he is about to show them how his miraculous new weapons operate, when the sage Nārada arrives and solemnly warns him: "Desist, O Arjuna! These mighty weapons should never be used, unless the need is very great. If you use them improperly, they will destroy the three worlds." As Arjuna puts up his weapons, the three worlds which had been trembling and quaking with terror, are calmed again (3.174).

The Pāṇḍu brothers continue to roam and on the Yamunā mountain they hear the story of the flood and how Manu, the first man, saved all living creatures from extinction by his kindness to a little fish who advised Manu to make a boat before the deluge came over the earth. The fish revealed himself as Brahma (185). Other stories are told purporting to demonstrate the greatness of Brahmans as a caste. One Brahman even learns self-control from a butcher in Mithilā.

Draupadī is then abducted by the Sindhu King Jayadratha, but her husbands recover her before he has gone very far (3.256). To console her, a visiting sage recounts the story of a woman who was in even greater distress than Draupadī, namely Sītā, the wife of Rāma, son of Daśaratha. When Sītā had been abducted by a demon and returned to her husband, he rejected her until the gods attested to her innocence [7] (3.257-76). Before the Pāṇḍavas leave the forest, they have an adventure that could well have been their last. One day, as they dwell nearby a hermitage, a priest's fire sticks get caught in a deer's antlers and are carried off into the forest. At the priest's request, the brothers pursue the animal all day until they collapse beneath a fig tree, completely exhausted and thirsty. Nakula climbs a tall tree to look for water. When he spots a grove of moisture-loving trees, he sets out until he comes to a pond of crystal-clear water. But just as he is about to drink, an unseen voice warns him not to touch the water before he has answered certain questions. Disregarding the request, Nakula drinks and falls dead on the ground. Yudhiṣṭhira then sends out the other brothers, one after the other, and they all meet with the same fate. When he goes himself and is summoned by the voice, he stops and declares himself willing to answer any questions. Then a Yakṣa, the master of the pond, identifies himself and asks Yudhiṣṭhira a set of riddles of a moral nature. Some of them are the following:

The Yakṣa: "What is it that makes the sun rise? Who accompanies him?"

Yudhiṣṭhira: "Brahma makes the sun rise, the gods keep him company, Dharma causes him to set and he is established in truth" (3.297.26-27).

The Yakṣa: "What is heavier than the earth itself? What is higher than the heavens? What is fleeter than the wind? And what is more numerous than grass-stalks?"

Yudhiṣṭhira: "A mother is heavier than the earth, a father is loftier than heaven, the mind is fleeter than the wind and our thoughts are more numerous than grass-stalks."

The Yakṣa: "What is it that does not shut its eyes when asleep? What does not move after its birth? What is without a heart? and what increases by its own momentum?"

Yudhiṣṭhira: "A fish does not close his eyes while asleep, an egg does not move after birth, a stone has no heart and a river increases by its own momentum."

The Yakṣa: "Who is the friend of the traveller? Who is the householder's friend? Who is the friend of the sick man? And who is the friend of one about to die?"

Yudhiṣṭhira: "The friends of a traveller in a distant country are his travel companions, the householder's friend is his wife, the physician is the sick man's friend and the friend of one who is about to die is charity" (40-45).

The Yakṣa: "What is man's self? What is the friend bestowed by god? What is his support? What is his highest refuge?"

Yudhiṣṭhira: "The son is a man's self, his wife is his friend given by god; rain is his means of support, giving is his highest goal" (50-51).

The Yakṣa: "What is the highest duty in the world? What is the ever rewarding duty? What is it one restrains without regret? With whom is an alliance not broken?"

Yudhiṣṭhira: "The highest duty is to refrain from injury. The virtue that ever rewards is the threefold duty. Restraining one's mind one does not feel regret. An alliance with good people is not broken."

The Yakṣa: "Renouncing what does one become agreeable? Renouncing what does one not repent? Renouncing what does one become wealthy and renouncing what does one become happy?"

Yudhiṣṭhira: "By renouncing pride one becomes agreeable, renouncing anger one does not feel sorry; by renouncing desire one becomes wealthy and by renouncing avarice, happy" (54-57).

The Yakṣa: "What is said to be the direction, what water, what food, O Pārtha, what poison? Name the time of a *śrāddha* 'religious ceremony' and then drink and take (water away)!"

Yudhiṣṭhira: "The good are the direction, space is water, the cow, food, a wish poison. A Brahman is the time for a *śrāddha.*"

The Yakṣa is satisfied with the answers. Finally he asks: "Tell me what a human being is and which man possesses everything." Yudhiṣṭhira replies: "As long as the report of one's good action touches heaven and earth and that report lasts, so long can one be called a human being. A man who regards comfort and discomfort, pleasure and pain, past and future as just the same, he is a man who has all possessions" (297.60-64).

In reward for his admirable replies, the Yakṣa offers to restore one of his brothers to life. To the Yakṣa's perplexity, Yudhiṣṭhira chooses Nakula, his half-brother. Yudhiṣṭhira explains that Nakula has another mother, and he considers it his duty to ensure that both mothers have surviving issue. The Yakṣa then revives the other brothers also, revealing himself as Dharma, the god of Duty, and Yudhiṣṭhira's father. Before disappearing he gives the brothers the fire sticks they had been hunting and grants them the boon of remaining unrecognized during the thirteenth year of their exile (3.298-99).

IV *At King Virāṭa's Court* (Virāṭa-parvan)

The Pāṇḍavas decide to spend the thirteenth year at the court of Virāṭa, King of the Matsyas, an old friend. Before entering the city they conceal their magic weapons in a bundle which they hang in a tree in a cemetery outside the city wall. To the onlooking shepherds and cowherds they explain that it is their mother's body. She had lived to be one hundred and eighty years old, and in accordance with their ancient customs they had placed the body in a tree. To disguise themselves they hire themselves out as servants to the court. Yudhiṣṭhira presents himself as an expert dice player and becomes the king's companion and counselor. Bhīma is employed as a cook, Nakula as a groom in the royal stables, and Sahadeva as a counter of cows. Arjuna becomes a transvestite, Bṛhannaḍā by name and is appointed dancing master for the girls of the court. Draupadī becomes the queen's hairdresser (4.1-11).

Their sojourn at the court passes uneventfully until Draupadī attracts the attention of Kīcaka, the commander of the army. In his propositions to her he claims that her beauty is going to waste: "Thou dost not display thy brilliance in spite of all thy loveliness, like a beautiful garland that lies unused. I shall leave my old wives; they must become your slaves, O sweet-smiling one, remaining ever obedient to thee, like slaves." Draupadī warns him that she is married already and that his conduct is improper. Her husbands are invisible Gandharvas who will think little of putting him to death. "Why do you desire me, O foolish Kīcaka; you act like a stupid baby on his mother's lap reaching for the moon." But Kīcaka does not give up and finally Draupadī resorts to a ruse whereby she promises the general a rendezvous in the middle of the night in the dancing hall. But when the ardent suitor comes, he does not find Draupadī in the dark dancing hall, but her husband Bhīma who kills him and breaks all the bones in his body. Draupadī is delighted and summons all the courtiers to come and see how her mighty husbands protect her (4.12-22).

Then Kīcaka's relatives stir up trouble. They insist that Draupadī by her compromising behavior deserves to be cremated together with her lover Kīcaka. Bhīma again comes to the rescue and in a terrible fight slays one hundred and five of the kinsmen with a tree he rips out of the ground. The frightened citizens demand the dismissal of Draupadī because she is a threat to the peace. The king upon her request grants her a thirteen-day reprieve. That is all the time remaining before the thirteenth year of the exile is expired (4.23).

Meanwhile, in Hāstinapura Duryodhana's spies report that their efforts to find the Pāṇḍavas are fruitless. The news of Kīcaka's death is received with joy, because Kurus and Matsyas are longtime enemies. They take this opportunity to join with another tribe, the Trigartas, in a cattle raid on Virāṭa's herds. First the Trigartas invade the country from the west, stealing hundreds and thousands of heads. When Virāṭa hears it, he marches out enlisting all the available manpower in the country, including Yudhiṣṭhira, Bhīma, Sahadeva, and Nakula. The Kurus take this opportunity to attack the deserted regions north of the city. The only man left in the city is Virāṭa's young son, scarcely more than a child, who courageously sets out to meet the enemy, taking the transvestite Bṛhannaḍā along as charioteer. Upon seeing the mighty Kuru army near the cemetery, the prince loses courage and jumps from the chariot pursued by Arjuna in his female disguise, much to the hilarity of the enemy. Arjuna recovers his priceless bow from the tree in the cemetery and blowing his horn Devadatta he storms at the Kurus who recoil in surprise and are soon driven off. Urging the prince not to betray his identity, Arjuna goes back to the capital where Virāṭa and the other Pāṇḍu brothers have meanwhile returned from a victory over the Trigartas. Three days later the thirteen years are over and the Pāṇḍavas reveal themselves to the astonished Virāṭa (4.24-66).

In gratitude for his services, the king offers Arjuna the hand of his daughter, but Arjuna accepts her only on behalf of his son Abhimanyu, out of consideration for the princess's reputation, now that it appears that she had been receiving dancing lessons from a man for a year. The wedding takes place with great pomp (4.67).

V *Preparations for the War* (Udyoga-parvan)

After the wedding, the princes friendly to Yudhiṣṭhira gather in the palace to consult on a course of action. Kṛṣṇa suggests that they send an envoy to Duryodhana to discover what his intentions are and to put forth the Pāṇḍavas' claim for half the kingdom. After various alternative proposals, they agree to send Drupada's court chaplain to Hāstinapura. Meanwhile, both Pāṇḍavas and Kurus are actively trying to enlist support and allies in the case of an armed conflict. Duryodhana and Arjuna approach Kṛṣṇa at exactly the same hour, while the latter is lying asleep, to ask him to join their respective camps. When Kṛṣṇa wakes up he is unwilling to commit himself, but states that one party can have his army and the other side himself as a noncombatant. Duryodhana chooses the army and Arjuna engages Kṛṣṇa as his private charioteer (5.1-7). Śalya, the twins' maternal uncle, joins Duryodhana's army, but secretly promises Arjuna that he will steer Karṇa's chariot in a manner favorable to Arjuna. Śalya finds time to justify his treacherous design by relating the story of Indra who had promised not to slay his enemy Vṛtra by day or by night, with weapons that are neither dry nor wet, stone nor wood, missiles nor clubs. Yet he kills Vṛtra at dusk with a mass of foam inspired by Viṣṇu (5.8-19).

Drupada's court chaplain arrives at Duryodhana's court where he sets forth the Pāṇḍavas' position, explaining that they seek a peaceful solution to the conflict. However, they demand their share of the kingdom and if Duryodhana is not willing to yield it amicably, then the Pāṇḍavas will have a huge army to back up their demands. King Dhṛtarāṣṭra, in turn, sends his own ambassador who merely states that the Kurus also want peace, but makes no positive offers. In sententious tones he advises Yudhiṣṭhira to overcome his anger and desist from maneuvers that might lead to war. Yudhiṣṭhira replies that he does not want war and that he is willing to forget all past insults and harassments, if the Kurus will return Indraprastha to him. Otherwise there will be war. Or else, let Dhṛtarāṣṭra give him only five villages, one for each of the brothers, and they will not fight. Bloodshed among relatives is to be avoided at all costs. They engage in a profound discussion, touching on the moral basis underlying the reasons for war, peace, and personal duty, in the end, the ambassador, Saṃjaya, goes back and berates Dhṛtarāṣṭra for his weakness. But the latter is ever under pressure from his belligerent son Duryodhana and brother-in-law, Śakuni. They refuse to change their minds (5.19-32). Unable to sleep, Dhṛtarāṣṭra has Vidura discourse to him on the morality of kings (5.33-41).

Then Kṛṣṇa appears in the Kuru camp to make another effort at a peaceful solution. He has been sent in spite of remonstrations from Draupadī who was thirsting for revenge for the injuries she had suffered: "Thirteen long years have I waited, nursing in my bosom that wrath like a smoldering fire. How can my heart be peaceful if I have not seen Duḥśāsana's dark arm writhing in the dust?" Kṛṣṇa is received solemnly at the capital, but his attempts to sway Duryodhana are fruitless. The latter states: "As long as I live, even as much land as can be covered by the point of a needle shall not pass from us to the Pāṇḍavas!" These proud, manly words serve only to exasperate Kṛṣṇa who inveighs against him in a tone so biting that Duḥśāsana begins to fear that the sentiment in the council chamber may turn against him and his brothers. With Duryodhana and the other brothers and their bellicose supporters, he walks out of the conference hall. After more pleas and frustrated negotiations, Kṛṣṇa gives up. He takes leave of the Pāṇḍavas' mother, Kuntī, who exhorts them to fight and then sets out on his return journey (5.89-137).

On his way back to the Pāṇḍavas, Kṛṣṇa is joined by Karṇa who explains to him the problem of his divided loyalty. He was born from Kuntī before she was married as a result of an encounter with the Sungod. For fear of shame she abandoned him when he was only an infant by floating him down the river in a little basket. He cannot forgive his mother for having rejected him. On the other hand, the Kurus have accepted him as one of their kind (see 1.126) and given him all the respect and recognition he is entitled to. Now, though he has moral scruples about fighting against his half-brothers, Duryodhana and his kin command his loyalty and support against aggression from any party, even his own close relatives. He will follow Duryodhana. With these words he leaves Kṛṣṇa and upon his return to the palace has a dramatic scene with his mother Kuntī, who tries to persuade him in high-flown language to join his brothers (5.138-44).

In the Pāṇḍava camp, old Bhīṣma has just reviewed all the incidents that led up to the conflict and also decides that his obedience lies with the king. Kṛṣṇa arrives with the report of the failure of his mission in spite of his supreme efforts to preserve the peace. Also, he announces that the enemy was preparing to march for Kurukṣetra, the plains of Kuru, in order to take up positions for the coming battle. Yudhiṣṭhira decides to meet them there and appoints generals to the seven armies he has at his disposal. The generals, together with Kṛṣṇa and the Pāṇḍu brothers, elect Dhṛṣṭadyumna, Draupadī's brother, as their commander-in-chief (5.145-48).

The Kurus, meanwhile, have appointed Bhīṣma to the post of commander-in-chief. He sums up the chariot fighters according to their skill and fitness in battle. Karṇa is deeply insulted when he is ranked lower than the other heroes and swears that he will not fight until Bhīṣma has fallen. The Kurus have eleven armies. Bhīṣma explains why he will fight all enemies except for one man, Śikhaṇḍin, because in a former life he had known him as a girl named Ambā. He relates her story: he had kidnapped her for his master, King Vicitravīrya. When she had refused to marry the king, he sent her off, but of course, by then she was unacceptable to any man, so that in despair she committed suicide, after having become part river, part human. Before she died, she vowed that in her next life she would avenge herself on Bhīṣma. Though reborn as a girl in Drupada's line, she later was miraculously transformed into a man, Śikhaṇḍin, by exchanging sexes with a Yakṣa. Śikhaṇḍin in consequence of her oath has joined the Pāṇḍava camp as a general of an army, but Bhīṣma still regards him as a woman and will not defend himself when attacked by him (5.149-193).

The Kurus set up a large battle front and behind it a vast encampment of supplies, provisions, camp followers and personnel, so that the area looks like a second Hāstinapura. The Pāṇḍavas confront them with a similar array of hundreds and thousands of foot soldiers, chariots, elephants and other war equipment (5.195-97). War is about to begin.

VI *Bhīṣma's Generalship* (Bhīṣma-parvan)

Before the outbreak of the battle, while the troops are aligned in opposing arrays on either side of the field of Kuru, the sage Vyāsa briefly appears to Dhṛtarāṣṭra and grants him a boon, namely, that Dhṛtarāṣṭra will be able to hear an account of the entire battle from the mouth of his charioteer Saṃjaya. The latter will be endowed with supernatural vision which enables him to observe every detail of the battle, whether concealed or apparent, and to report it to his blind lord (6.1-2).

Saṃjaya first gives a colorful sketch of the geography of the land of the Bhāratas and its inhabitants (6.5-13). In the next scene, he returns from the battlefield after Bhīṣma has been slain and he commences to narrate in detail all the incidents that took place while he was in the fray.

He begins the account of the battle with a lively description of the noise and tumult attendant upon the waking up and marching of the two armies, "like flamingos crossing a great lake," cheerfully shouting and blowing their musical instruments. Bhīṣma, the army chief and venerable granduncle of the Kurus assembles his generals and addresses them with encouraging words: "Here is, O Kṣatriyas, the great gate of heaven standing wide open for you. Enter ye through it into the realms of Indra and Brahma! It is the warrior's eternal duty to die in battle, not to meet his end at home." On the Pāṇḍu side, King Yudhiṣṭhira spurs on his warriors in similar terms and with Arjuna in the central army, the mighty force moves forward, eagerly anticipating the clash of arms. Saṃjaya lists the names and tribes composing the hostile armies and their valiant leaders (6.14-22).

At that point Arjuna in his chariot wavers. He is suddenly overcome by the realization that he is about to fight his own kinsmen and that to win the battle signifies no more than the death and annihilation of his close relatives and the prospect of a postwar reputation as a parricide. Tortured by these disturbing thoughts he sinks down in his chariot, impotent, announcing to his charioteer, Kṛṣṇa, that he will not fight. Kṛṣṇa encourages him with compelling arguments until he has recovered from his depression. Kṛṣṇa's speech is contained in the so-called *Bhagavad-gītā* "Song of the exalted one," of which an excerpt follows: Arjuna has just explained his conscientious objection against the battle and ends:

For I do not see what would dispel the sorrow that would be searing my senses should I achieve a prosperous dominion on earth without rivals, yes, even overlordship of the gods (24.8).

The Exalted One spoke: You grieved about people who need not be mourned and do you speak words of wisdom? Neither for the dead, nor for those who have not died yet do the wise mourn. But in no respect was I ever not, nor you, nor these kings of people, nor, indeed, shall we ever not come to be, all of us, henceforward. Just as the embodied soul in this body passes through childhood, youth, old age, so too will it obtain another body; a wise man does not become perplexed in this matter. But contacts with matter, O son of Kuntī, produce cold and heat, pleasure and pain; they come and go, are ephemeral; bear up with them, O scion of Bhārata! For the man whom these (contacts) do not shake, O bull among men, to whom pain and pleasure are the same, who is steadfast, he is fit for immortality. Of that which is not, no coming into being takes place, nor a not coming into being of that which is; but the nature of both these is seen by those that see the truth. But know that that by which all this is pervaded, is indestructible; the destruction of this imperishable one nobody can perpetrate. These bodies of the eternal embodied one are said to come to an end, of that indestructible, immeasurable one; therefore, fight, O scion of Bhārata! (24.11-18)

Just as a man discarding his old garments puts on other, new ones, so the embodied one enters into other, new bodies, having discarded the worn-out ones. Weapons do not cut him, fire does not burn him, nor does water wet him, nor wind dry him. This one is uncuttable, unburnable, not to be wet and not to be dried either, eternal omnipresent, fixed, immobile, everlasting (24.22-24).

Kṛṣṇa continues to hold forth in this vein. Close to a nervous crisis as he is, Arjuna is willing to accept Kṛṣṇa's teachings and asks how the latter reconciles his doctrines of action and violence with the often contradictory philosophical trends of his time, Sāñkhya and Yoga. Kṛṣṇa explains that he is an incarnation of the Supreme Deity and embodies all that has ever existed and will exist. In a mystic vision Arjuna then beholds Kṛṣṇa's immortal self: "Behold, O Pārtha (Arjuna), my forms by hundreds and thousands, of various sorts, divine and possessed of various hues and aspects" (33.5). "If suddenly the light of a thousand suns in the sky should burst forth, then the blaze would be equal to that of the Exalted One" (33.12). In a rapturous speech Arjuna describes what he sees: the whole universe with all the gods is in Kṛṣṇa who at the same time appears as a radiant image of Viṣṇu, timeless, imperishable, praised by seers and gods. Then Kṛṣṇa appears in his frightful aspect, as the God of Death with horrible tusks, destroying the world and devouring people, among them Dhṛtarāṣṭra's sons. So since the latter are virtually dead, Arjuna need not hesitate to slay them on the battlefield. Prostrating himself, Arjuna worships his Lord and continues to listen devoutly, until he can declare: "My confusion is obliterated, I have gained something to remember by Thy grace, O Changeless One. I am standing firm, my doubts resolved. I shall do what Thou sayest" (40.73).

For the next eighteen days, the parties fight a wearisome, bloody battle, only interrupted by the coming of night.

For the first ten days, Bhīṣma is in command. The first day witnesses a combat between Bhīṣma and Abhimanyu which remains undecided. One of the first casualties is Virāṭa's youthful son (see 4.35) who is killed by Śalya after he had killed Śalya's four horses. Bhīṣma succeeds in routing Arjuna after a murderous exchange of arrows. When Bhīṣma attacks the soldiery, he "fells the heads of the car warriors like a skillful man throwing down ripe fruit from a tree. And the heads of those warriors, O King, fall down upon the ground with thudding noises, resembling a hail of rocks" (6.82.21ff.). Bhīma kills numerous sons of Dhṛtarāṣṭra who tumble from their chariots like mangoes (6.43-46).

On the second day of the battle Bhīṣma continues his duel with Arjuna, while Dhṛṣṭadyumna is engaged by Droṇa. Having killed his opponent's charioteer, Droṇa intercepts his dart and mace by skillfully shattering them in the air. When Bhīma intercedes, Droṇa shifts his ground leaving the King of the Kaliṅgas to fight Bhīma. Impetuously, the mighty hero fighting on the ground makes "a river to flow with a bloody current full of gore and flesh of the warriors born in Kaliṅga." Before the morning is over the Kaliṅgas have been destroyed. The Kuru army cannot maintain its position and is about to be routed when Bhīṣma orders it to retire for the night (6.47-51).

In the free-for-all taking place on the third day, the armies slaughter each other terribly. "Hosts of soldiers by the hundreds of thousands were felled by cavalry and cavalry by infantry . . . Innumerable headless trunks arose all around signaling the end of the world." The Kuru kings band together to slay Arjuna, but he is a match for them even when Bhīṣma joins the fray. Kṛṣṇa grows so impatient that he jumps from the chariot and throws his discus at Bhīṣma without hurting him, however. Arjuna has to drag him back to the chariot (6.52-55).

On the fourth day the fighting continues as before. Bhīsma slays ten thousand elephants with his mace after withstanding a charge of the Māgadhas. Their bodies lie around like hills rent by lightning while Bhīṣma moves through the scene of slaughter, his mace wet with blood, like Śiva the destroyer of the universe. Later, two arrows put him out of condition for some time (6.56-60). The next day, the battle continues, revolving around a duel between Arjuna and Bhīṣma. Arjuna by the end of the day has killed twenty-five thousand great charioteers (6.65-70). The battle is resumed on the sixth day. Dhṛṣṭadyumna and Bhīma engage Droṇa and his army, but are about to be repelled when Abhimanyu comes to their support, rushing in with such force that the opposite army "was unable to remain intact and reeled back, overcome as it was, like a drunken woman in the street, by confusion and stupefaction." In spite of Droṇa's exhortations, the Kurus fall back pursued by the Pāṇḍava army who perpetrate such a slaughter that "the battlefield resembled an ocean whose water was blood, whose whirlpools were chariots, whose islands were elephants and whose waves were horses." Nightfall interrupts the raging battle (6.71-76). The seventh day sees little change. The Pāṇḍava brothers excel in their individual combats with Bhīṣma, but fail to kill him. The next day Bhīma succeeds in felling Bhīṣma's charioteer whereupon the horses carry him off. Bhīma then slays eight of Dhṛtarāṣṭra's sons, and the remainder flee. Bhīṣma meanwhile is reproached by Duryodhana for not exerting enough effort in killing the Pāṇḍavas. He apologizes arguing that the Pāṇḍavas are going to win anyway. When Bhīma slays seven more of Dhṛtarāṣṭra's sons, the earth is said to "shine, strewn as it was with the arms anointed with sandal paste, covered by leather fences and bracelets, with the hewn-off thighs resembling the trunks of elephants of the energetic warriors and with the bejewelled, severed heads carrying diadems and ear-rings, of the bull-eyed ones" (6.77-93).

At the end of the ninth day, Yudhiṣṭhira complains that Bhīṣma is raising havoc among his troops. Kṛṣṇa and the brothers decide to go to Bhīṣma to ask him in what manner he may be killed. They cross to the enemy camp and Bhīṣma readily replies that he can vanquish every warrior except Śikhaṇḍin (see 5.170), because the latter is a woman. The next day, in the fierce battle, Arjuna moves closer to Bhīṣma all the time using Śikhaṇḍin as a shield. Śikhaṇḍin starts harassing Bhīṣma with arrows without much effect. Only when under the cover of Śikhaṇḍin, Arjuna shoots hundreds of arrows into Bhīṣma, does the latter collapse and fall from his chariot. The earth trembles and rain falls. He is so skewered with arrows that his body does not touch the ground and to provide him with a head support, a "warrior's cushion," as he calls it, Arjuna shoots three arrows into the ground to rest Bhīṣma's head on. He remains alive until after the battle, when a time auspicious for his death arrives (6.95-117).

VII *Droṇa's Generalship* (Droṇa-parvan)

After Bhīṣma's fall, friend and foe alike pay their respects to the grand-sire. To Karṇa Bhīṣma speaks conciliatory words: "Like the ocean with respect to rivers, like the sun in respect to all other shining bodies, like a fertile soil in respect to seeds, like the clouds in respect to creatures, be thou (O Karṇa), the refuge for thy relatives and friends." Later Karṇa proposes to appoint Droṇa as their commander-in-chief (7.1-6).

The next day, the twelfth of the battle, Droṇa outlines a strategy to capture Yudhiṣṭhira, but due to the tremendous opposition from other warriors, he never gets close to him and the plan fails. Many other combats take place. Bhīma kills an elephant with his bare hands (7.16-31). On the morning of the next day Duryodhana derides Droṇa for not having seized Yudhiṣṭhira. Droṇa is dejected. The Kurus band together to attack Arjuna's son Abhimanyu. He wards off all his opponents, until Karṇa destroys his bow and kills his side-runners and horses. Forced to fight on the ground, Abhimanyu is surrounded by hosts of hostile chariot fighters who soon deprive him of his weapons. They continue to pour shafts into him until he looks like a porcupine. Powerless, but true to his heroic code of resistance to the very end, Abhimanyu fights on until one of the enemies deals him a fatal blow with a huge mace. As he lay dead on the field he looked like an extinguished fire in the summer, after it has ravaged a whole forest. The Kurus are gleeful, but Arjuna is filled with bitterness and self-reproach (7.32-49).

On the fourteenth day of the battle many fierce combats take place. Bhīma puts Karṇa to flight with his arrows, but he soon returns and after a bitter fight forces Bhīma to abandon his chariot. He now has Bhīma at his mercy, but mindful of a promise to Kuntī, he does not kill him, but merely prods him with the horn end of his bow, insulting him all the while, until Arjuna chases him away. Arjuna then proceeds to slay King Jayadratha who once so shamefully had kidnapped Draupadī (see 3.256). Arjuna severs his head with a razor-sharp arrow. That night the warriors do not return to their camps, but continue to fight by the unearthly glow of torch-lights. Ghaṭotkaca is killed by Karṇa who had to resort to a never failing dart that Indra had given him and so doing, forfeited it (7.58-154).

Exhausted by the all-night battle, the warriors fall asleep in their chariots and on the elephants, but soon the dawn breaks and the battle starts afresh. This day Droṇa falls by a tricky stratagem employed by Yudhiṣṭhira. The latter is known for his truthfulness, so when he calls out to Droṇa that Aśvatthāman is dead, Droṇa believes that his son has just been killed. In despair he throws down his weapons. In fact, Bhīma had just slain a big elephant named Aśvatthāman and Kṛṣṇa had urged Yudhiṣṭhira to cry out this half-truth. In an attempt to avoid telling a lie, Yudhiṣṭhira adds in an undertone—"the elephant!"—but fate cannot be deceived and Yudhiṣṭhira who had been so truthful that his chariot wheels never touched the ground, now rides like other mortals. Dhṛṣṭadyumna cuts off Droṇa's head in revenge for his father's humiliation (see 1.154) (7.165-73).

VIII *Karṇa's Generalship* (Karṇa-parvan)

On the sixteenth day, Karṇa is elected commander-in-chief and, after some protest, Śalya agrees to be his charioteer. He has a long exchange of insults with Karṇa. The battle rages on all day. At one point Karṇa manages to disarm Yudhiṣṭhira, but again, he does not kill him but pats him on the shoulder remarking sarcastically that he is a better student than warrior and should stay away from conflicts with real heroes. Later Yudhiṣṭhira confesses to Arjuna how much he hates Karṇa because of his boasting and uncouth manners (8.46.16-17). Then he angrily asks Arjuna why he has not slain him yet. Filled with rage, Arjuna would have attacked him, were it not for Kṛṣṇa's intervention. The brothers embrace and have a dramatic reconciliation (8.1-50).

Challenged by Duḥśāsana, Bhīma rushes at him and hurls his terrible mace, knocking him from the car. He jumps after him and thinking of the insults he has had to endure from Duḥśāsana, he "drew his exceedingly terrible, sharp sword and placing his foot on the trembling man, at the neck, he ripped open the breast of the fallen one and then drank his tepid blood" (8.61.6). Next Arjuna pursues Karṇa, who is in a rage because his son has just been killed. After a long, gruesome fight in which each resorts to his divine weapons several times, a wheel of Karṇa's chariot gets lodged in the ground and he cannot move it. Shedding tears of frustration, he shouts at Arjuna: "O Pārtha, hold off from an intention practised by cowards only. Heroes do not shoot at a person whose hair is disarranged, who faces another direction, who is a Brahman, a suppliant, a refugee . . . nor at one whose weapons are broken or lost in battle. . . . And you, O Arjuna, are a hero; therefore, wait for just a moment until I pull this wheel out, O winner of wealth! Standing on a chariot you are not supposed to kill me, as I am out of combat. I fear neither Kṛṣṇa nor you, O Arjuna, for you hail from a warrior race, you are a perpetuator of a noble family. Remember the precepts of our caste duty, O Pāṇḍava, and wait for a moment!" But his pleas are to no avail. In a caustic speech Kṛṣṇa asks him whether Karṇa observed his caste duty when he insulted Draupadī, or forced the inexperienced Yudhiṣṭhira to gamble with a gamester as skilled as Śakuni. With a well-aimed arrow launched from his mighty bow Gāṇḍiva, Arjuna severed Karṇa's head which fell to the ground like the thousand-rayed sun at the close of the day (8.66-67).

IX *Śalya's Generalship* (Śalya-parvan)

On the final day, Śalya is chosen as leader. He does not survive very long, being soon struck down by the Yudhiṣṭhira's magic weapon. Duryodhana appoints himself general, but his army cannot withstand the onslaught and flees. Duryodhana hides in a lake, but he is again caught by the Pāṇḍavas. He undertakes to fight a duel to death with Bhīma, choosing the mace as weapon. After a long, grim battle, Bhīma with a terrible blow smashes his opponent's thigh whereupon Duryodhana falls to the ground, senseless, though not yet dead. Full of hatred and rancor, Bhīma kicks his head with his left foot, an act that shocks the bystanders. The Kuru army has been annihilated, but for three knights, Kṛpa, Kṛtavarman, and Droṇa's son Aśvatthāman.

X *The Nocturnal Raid* (Sauptika-parvan)

The three surviving Kuru knights repair for the night to a dense forest. A few hours later they stealthily enter the camp of the Pāṇḍavas where the victorious army is at rest, except for the Pāṇḍu brothers and Kṛṣṇa, who have gone to the capital. Mercilessly, the three Kuru warriors massacre all the soldiers in their sleep and then set fire to the camp. Afterward, they visit Duryodhana to report the news. He blesses them gratefully and breathes his last (10.1-9).

Here Saṃjaya's account of the battle ends. [The *Mahābhārata* continues for another eight books, which contain the greater part of the philosophical material.]

XI *The Women* (Strī-parvan)

Now that the battle is over the disconsolate widows of the soldiers visit the bleak, deserted battlefield, wailing and lamenting. Dhṛtarāṣṭra also comes and is grief stricken by the loss of one hundred sons. To console him, Vidura relates to him the story of the Man in the Well:

"A certain twice-born, abiding in the cycle of existence, as I have heard, arrived in an impassable, great forest full of carnivores, everywhere teeming with very horrible, voracious (beings), resembling lions, tigers and elephants, producing dread in Death itself. Having seen that, his heart gave way to great trepidation; his very hair rose" . . . He looks for an escape, but lands in "a horrible forest, covered everywhere with traps and nets. A very horrible woman embraced it with her arms. The great forest was teeming with five-headed snakes which raised themselves like rocks (and) with great trees that touched the sky. And there was in the middle of that forest a concealed well, entirely covered with invisible vines, hidden as they were by grass. That twice-born fell into that hidden abode of water and was hung up in that interlacing tangle of creepers, as if he had become a big fruit, attached by its stalk, of the breadfruit tree. Thus he hangs there, his feet up and his head down. And then a further calamity befell him (there): on the circular masonry of the well he saw a great elephant having six mouths, spotted black, moving on twelve feet, approaching slowly, covered with vines and trees. And on its (a tree's) branches, horrible in form, terrifying, were sitting bees who had just brought honey. More and more they endeavoured to collect honey, O bull among men, which is the sweetest thing in which even a fool among creatures takes pleasure. Streams of that honey flowed everywhere, then, and his thirst was not allayed as he was drinking, in his danger. He desired it all the time, unsatiated time and again. And he did not become disgusted with life. White and black mice gnawed at the tree."

The parable is explained as follows: The forest is *saṃsāra,* the creepers are diseases, the woman is old age, the well is the human body, the snake is time, the vine from which the man was hanging is hope in life, the elephant is the year, his twelve feet the months, the mice are nights and days, the bees desires, the streams of honey are the enjoyment of desire in which human beings sink away (11.5-6).

Next, Yudhiṣṭhira and his brothers visit the bereft ladies and old King Dhṛtarāṣṭra on the battlefield. It is their first meeting after the carnage of the great war and becomes an emotional scene marked by mutual recriminations. Dhṛtarāṣṭra crushes with his hands an iron image that he believes is Bhīma. Yudhiṣṭhira calculates how many millions of combatants have perished. They all weep, and in the end Kuntī, in a tearful voice, confesses to Arjuna for the first time that Karṇa had been his brother (11.7-27).

XII *Peace* (Śānti-parvan)

The war is over and the Pāṇḍava brothers sit around Bhīṣma who is lying on his bed of arrows answering philosophical questions put to him by Yudhiṣṭhira. Yudhiṣṭhira's questions are brief but the replies he gets are lengthy and often obscure. In the first part of the Book of Peace (Ch. 1-129), Bhīṣma replies to questions on the morality of kingship (*Rājadharma*), explaining the legal and moral foundations of kingship, how a just king rules and what he ought to do and avoid doing. In the second part, called *Āpaddharma,* "morality in adversity," Bhīṣma expounds the proper course of action during times of distress. In the third and last part of the book (Chs. 168-353), he deals with the problem of release, or liberation from the bonds of earthly existence (*Mokṣadharma*). Extracts of each of these parts will be found below in Chapter 6. The Mokṣadharma is of particular interest because it contains many doctrines that have become part of the great Hindu tradition. The following enumeration is only a sample of many topics discussed.

Bhīṣma teaches that enlightened, self-imposed poverty is a more certain way to attain happiness than wealth. He also expounds a theory of the origin of caste in some detail (12.181-82 and 282-83) (see p. 60). One should not sleep late, nor pass urine while facing the sun (12.186). The sect of mutterers is referred to who by their muttering (*japa-*) attempt to gain salvation (12.192). Sexual desire may be sublimated by the following scheme: desire produces semen in the body which is carried upward to the head by one of thousands of ducts, called *manovahā*. It spills the semen again upon arousal. One can achieve release by concentrating all the life-breaths into this duct, *manovahā,* upon death (12.207). Dreams are manifestations of actions performed in a previous life which have produced either happiness or misery[8] (12.209). King Janaka of Mithilā, also known from Buddhist scriptures, questions a Sāṅkhya philosopher on the nature of the soul (12.211). Epic time divisions are summed up as follows: one day and night are subdivided as thirty *muhūrtas*. Each *muhūrta* consists of 30 ¼ *kalās* "portions"; every *kalā* lasts thirty *kāṣṭhās* "marks," and fifteen winks of the eye make up one *kāṣṭhā*. Thirty days and nights form one month and twelve months one year. *Yugas* "eras" are measured in years (12.224).

Several times emphasis is laid on abstaining from sacrificing animals (12.254ff.). Capital punishment is examined from an ethical point of view, and it is concluded that in some circumstances it is necessary (12.259). The creatures of the world owe their ailments and fever to drops of perspiration from Śiva's brow which fell when he was pursuing a sacrificed animal that had run away from him (12.274). A man should be devoted to his elders, especially when they have passed on. After one dies, one's spirit roams around like a cloud for some time. Many types of death exist and each has a different effect on rebirth. Suicide is wrong. Cremation is necessary (12.286).

Stories relating the greatness of Brahmans are numerous. Indra is cursed by a Brahman Gautama to grow a green beard because he has seduced Gautama's wife Ahalyā; he lost his testicles as a result of another Brahman's curse. Śiva's forehead is disfigured by a third eye due to the ascetic power of a Brahman. The sage Triśiras is angered at the gods and by his magic grows to enormous proportions. With one mouth he drinks all the sacrificial soma, with another he eats offerings, and with a third he prepares to swallow the gods. In great fear they fashion a thunderbolt from the bones of a Brahman, Dadhīci. The latter suffers himself to be killed for this purpose, and the monster is slain. The moon bears a mark, the hare-mark, because of the curse of a Brahman. The Himālayas do not produce gems because they had been cursed by a Brahman (12.329). The book ends with an account of a searcher of the highest good who is told by a Brahman that he should strive to become like a shining being that he had once observed, brilliant as the sun. This was the soul of a Brahman who had strictly observed a vow to glean food only (*uñchavṛtti*) (12.352).

The remaining sections of the Book of Peace are almost wholly philosophical and cosmogonical. From a historical point of view they contain some of the most interesting episodes of the *Mahābhārata*. Little can be gained from an enumeration of the various philosophical dialogues and their arguments in the Book of Peace. They are often tediously monotonous and repetitious with their admonitions for a proper life, and also their arguments presuppose some familiarity with the categories of Indian philosophy. These will be considered in Chapter 5.

XIII *Instruction* (Anuśāsana-parvan)

The same as has been said for the *Mokṣadharma* section of the Book of Peace holds for the Book of Instruction. It is a concatenation of discourses, dialogues, anecdotes and sermons which follow one another with a relentless singleness of purpose, to instill the proper morality into the listener. In the tragic context of the Epic story it seems cruel to experience a feeling of relief when at the end of this book Bhīṣma breathes his last and is cremated with the proper rites on the bank of the River Ganges, his mother.

XIV *The Horse-sacrifice* (Āśvamedhika-parvan)

Next, to atone for his sins and those of his brothers, Yudhiṣthira undertakes a horse sacrifice.[9] Before Kṛṣṇa returns to his own country, Dvārakā, he repeats to Arjuna a discourse on morality, the structure of the universe, and so on, called the *Anugītā* "Later Song" (14.16-50), later, that is, relative to the *Bhagavadgītā*. On his way home Kṛṣṇa meets the ascetic Uttañka in the desert of Maru, who receives a boon from Kṛṣṇa to have water wherever he wants. When Uttañka subsequently meets a tribesman who offers him urine to drink, he recoils in disgust, until the man identifies himself as Indra and the urine as soma (14.51-55).

Yudhiṣṭhira pays for his sacrifice by unearthing a large hidden treasure in the Himālayas. The horse returns to the capital and is cut into pieces according to the age-old rituals that make the sacrifice powerful. Its marrow is burned in the sacrificial fire and by smelling its smoke, the Pāṇḍavas are cleansed of all sins. The chief officiant, Vyāsa, receives many treasures, but gives them to Kuntī, his daughter-in-law (14.1-91).

Arjuna has a son Parikṣit who is stillborn, but is revived by Kṛṣṇa on the strength of an oath that he had never pronounced a falsehood [10] (14.65-68). The sacrifice is completed with great solemnity.

XV *The Sojourn at the Hermitage* (Āśramavāsika-parvan)

In this book, Dhṛtarāṣṭra and his wife Gāndhārī, unable to bear Bhīma's insolent taunts, retire to a forest hermitage. Kuntī joins them. Later they are visited by the Pāṇḍavas. After their arrival, Dhṛtarāṣṭra who still mourns his sons, is granted a vision of his deceased children and kinsmen through the grace of Vyāsa. All warriors in full battle dress appear before their eyes from a river, as if they were alive or painted on a canvas. Soon the dead mix with the living conversing and playing joyfully all night long, until the break of day. After the vision, many of the warriors' widows drown themselves in the river to join their husbands (15.1-14).

Two years later the elderly couple and Kuntī perish in a forest fire. Fortunately, the fire had been started through the negligence of some sacrificing Brahmans, so that in effect the three old people lost their lives in a sacrificial fire.

XVI *The Iron Club* (Mausala-parvan)

The next three books are tragic in character, describing the end of the heroic age and the dissolution of the powerful Kuru state. Yudhiṣṭhira learns that in far-off Dvārakā the race to which Kṛṣṇa belongs, has been exterminated. The sad affair began as a joke when a number of noisy youths of Kṛṣṇa's clan dressed up his son Sāmba as a pregnant woman and took him to a conclave of serious sages asking them to guess whether the offspring would be male or female. Furious at this attempt at deception the sages pronounced a curse that a terrible iron club would be born to Sāmba which would destroy the races of Vṛṣṇis and Andhakas. The King of the Vṛṣṇis was determined to frustrate the calamity, so when the fierce iron mace was born the next day, he had it pulverized and thrown into the ocean. But to no avail: from the powdered iron grew a grass called *Sāveraka* which would play a role in the oncoming disaster.

Frightened by evil omens, the Andhakas and Vṛṣṇis set out for a holy watering place. The first night they camped along the coast and began to drink spirituous liquor. Soon all were so drunk that they committed various outrages, such as insulting one another and giving away food to monkeys, rather than to Brahmans. The drunken orgy soon turned into a brawl which led to a wild scene, as the two clans fought each other to death. Kṛṣṇa had remained a passive bystander until he saw his own son killed. Then he picked up a handful of *sāveraka* grass that was growing along the shore and joined the melee. In his hands every blade of grass turned into a frightful iron mace. Only when the remainder of the two clans had been wiped out did he rest. He then withdrew into a forest and sat down to meditate. A passing hunter called *Jarā* "old age," mistook him for a deer and shot a fatal arrow into his foot. Kṛṣṇa died and ascended to heaven and thus Viṣṇu's *avatāra* came to an end (16.1-5).

Arjuna grieves, but Vyāsa tells him: "Almighty time is the root of all that takes place: it lowers the mighty and elevates the humble, it makes master into slave and servant into ruler. And Time has also come to end your life, O Arjuna."

XVII *The Great Departure* (Mahāprasthānika-parvan)

Now the Pāṇḍu brothers and Draupadī set out for their final journey. They first circumambulate the world, then proceed northward until one after the other, Draupadī, Sahadeva, Nakula, Arjuna, and Bhīma fall down dead.[11] Yudhiṣṭhira is fetched in Indra's chariot, but not until he has insisted that his faithful dog should come along, against Indra's objections. Yudhiṣṭhira pleads so convincingly, that the dog is admitted to heaven.

XVIII *The Ascent to Heaven* (Svargārohaṇa-parvan)

In this book we see Yudhiṣṭhira entering heaven. Appalled at seeing all his enemies frolicking happily, he demands another heaven but is instead guided to a terrible hell. It is a dark place polluted by blood, abounding in flies, stinging insects, rotting corpses, with forests of trees whose leaves are razors, hot plains, and boiling rivers. The celestial car stops and from a distance he hears the moaning voices of his brothers calling out to him. Enraged and baffled by the injustice of the gods, he tells his charioteer that he prefers to stay with his brothers rather than enjoy happiness with his former enemies. But it turns out to be a test for Yudhiṣṭhira's moral strength. The hell is illusory and soon he finds himself surrounded by his friends and loved ones who have all become deities such as they were before, or have become united with their parent gods (18.1-5).

Here ends the narrative of the battle of the Bhāratas. In the last chapter of this huge, encyclopedic work, the advantages and moral merits which one gains from perusing it, are recounted. "That he who reads the *Mahābhārata* story with due application should go to supreme felicity—I do not doubt that" (18.5-53).

CHAPTER 3

Structure and Contents of the Mahābhārata

THIS chapter will examine in more detail some of the features of the *Mahābhārata* relating to its form, style, language, and content, as well as attempt to define its position in Sanskrit literature. References will be made to the Epic story as related in Chapter 2, or to the Sanskrit original.

I *Origins*

Historically, very little is known about the *Mahābhārata.* The grammarian Pāṇini (fourth century B.C.?) teaches the formation of the word *Mahābhārata.*[1] The Vedic literature has no references to it, and so chronologically it comes after the *Vedas* and before the *Purāṇas,* who quote from it. It is probably contemporary with the later *Upaniṣads,* the Lawbooks and the *Arthaśāstra.* It is not a sacred work in the sense the *Vedas* are, so no necessity existed to preserve its text literally.

The supposed author of the *Mahābhārata* is the mythical saint Vyāsa, also called Kṛṣṇa Dvaipāyana, who was the natural grandfather of the heroes and witnessed the battle. He is also said to have arranged the *Vedas,* hence his name *Vyāsa* "arranger." Other works are also credited to his authorship, but he remains a mythological figure whose historicity may well be doubted.

Then how did the *Mahābhārata* originate? This problem has been the subject of many learned discussions and at least half a dozen solutions have been offered, all ultimately speculative, but some adhering closer to the facts than others. Early investigators, unable to reconcile the strictly epic with the didactic passages, maintained that the two could not have come from the same pen and so attempted to dissect the Epic along these lines. If the nucleus was a historical event, it must have been the battle of the Bhāratas which gave inspiration to an epic poem, just as the Trojan war inspired Homer's *Iliad*. Efforts were made to "reconstruct" this original poem. The Danish scholar Sören Sörensen (1893) who postulated that the original Epic did not contain contradictions or irrelevant digressions, was able to trim it down to a poem of about eight thousand stanzas, from a text of about ninety-five thousand. Adolf Holtzmann, a German investigator, invented a theory that explained a curious contradiction in the *Mahābhārata,* namely that the heroes are apt to practice deceit and fraud, whereas their opponents fight according to the accepted rules of battle. Holtzmann's "inversion theory" held that in the original Epic the Kuru kings and not the Pāṇḍavas were the heroes, but that descendants of the victorious Pāṇḍus ordered their court poets to rewrite the popular battle story.[2] Other scholars elaborated on or supported this theory. It has little to recommend it, however, as it raises more problems than it solves.

Some scholars believe that the Epic was the work of one man. This "one-author" theory was first proposed by the Jesuit priest Joseph Dahlmann. According to him, a single inspired poet reworked a number of existing stories, sagas, and lawbooks into a huge single work with the aim of providing the masses with standards of law and justice in a popular form. In his view, the battle story need not have had any historical basis, but could just as well be a symbolic representation of the battle between good and evil.[3] The French scholar Sylvain Lévi even saw the *Bhagavad-gītā* as the central theme around which a poet had woven the epic story of Pāṇḍavas and Kurus with the aim of popularizing the Bhāgavata faith.[4] The "one-author" theory is at least in agreement with the statement of the *Mahābhārata* itself, although it ignores the striking variations in style, language, and versification in the different parts of the Epic.

The American scholar E. Washburn Hopkins was the most articulate spokesman for a third explanation which can be called the "analytic" theory.[5] Struck by the great dissimilarities in diction, meter, language, and tone of the various parts of the Epic, Hopkins proposed that the *Mahābhārata* is a compilation consisting of various layers which have been grafted onto an original core in the course of the Epic's evolution from a comparatively small collection of lays to its present bulk. He believes the original to have started as a set of hymns of praise sung by priests to glorify their royal patron, in about 400 B.C.

Between 400 and 200 B.C. the *Mahābhārata* began to emerge as a heroic tale with the Pāṇḍus as heroes and Kṛṣṇa as a demigod. In the next three or four hundred years, Kṛṣṇa rose to the status of a universal god and masses of didactic material were inserted. Between A.D. 200 and 400, the *Anuśāsana* grew to such proportions that it was separated from the *Śānti* and recognized as a separate book. In this period also, the last books were added and the introduction to the first book.

This theory conforms to the facts that Hopkins has gathered about the origin of the *Mahābhārata,* namely, that in its present form, even without its didactic material, the Epic was composed before Alexander's invasion (325 B.C.). All the moral and didactic material which Hopkins elsewhere refers to as the "pseudo-epic," was inserted later on. The *Mahābhārata* was not essentially a Kṛṣṇaite religious work until somewhere near the first century B.C. It was practically completed by A.D. 200, but no precise date can be given for the entire Epic. The facts Hopkins adduces cannot very well be disputed. Also, the mechanism he postulates for the accretion of epic material over the years, is quite credible. Exactly similar additions to later, regional versions of the *Mahābhārata* have been identified lately by purely objective, textcritical methods. Hopkins' analytic theory is, therefore, widely accepted. One crucial flaw in its application, however, is the impossibility of ascertaining whether any given passage of the epic is older or later in origin. Hopkins often guessed and guessed wrongly. So far, no satisfactory objective criteria have been set up.

Passing over some theories proposed by other scholars, we shall turn directly to the viewpoint of one of the most eminent of *Mahābhārata* interpreters, Dr. V. S. Sukthankar.[6] He is not immediately concerned with the historical origin of the *Mahābhārata,* but is an exponent of the typically holistic appreciation of its narrative and meaning. Sukthankar distinguishes three levels on which the Epic story takes place: a "mundane," an "ethical," and a "metaphysical." Deprecating the efforts of analytical minds to search for the nucleus of the Epic, he instead, focuses on its "inner meaning," its symbolism. The physical battle is really a battle of good gods versus evil demons on the "ethical" level, and at the same time it is symbolic of the struggle for supremacy of our mental faculties, the base versus the high. But a holistic approach again presumes a singular authorship, which like Dahlmann's theory, does not account satisfactorily for the striking heterogeneity of the *Mahābhārata.* Perhaps we have to assume that the person responsible for the final recension incorporated narratives into the Epic which he did not compose himself and tried to give a metaphysical purposefulness to the story which was not found there before. Or perhaps, we ought to take to heart a Jain account of the legend of Vyāsa:

> Vyāsa knew that his poem is full of lies, but he ventured to make it known after the following experiment: He placed a pot on the bank of the Ganges and began to heap sand over it. Immediately, people came along and followed his example, so that after a short time the place where the first pot had stood could no longer be determined at all. Since people so readily carry out a senseless work, he thought, nobody would find contradictions in his work.[7]

II *Structure*

The *Mahābhārata* is a frame story, a set of narratives which are nested like Chinese balls one within the other. This form is common in Indian literature, as it is in many literatures outside India. The main story is contained in three layers. The person whose words we hear in the Naimiṣa forest is the Sūta, the bard, as he speaks to a conclave of Brahmans attending Janamejaya's Twelve-year sacrifice. His narrative ends at the very end of the last book and constitutes the outer shell. The second shell begins when the Sūta introduces Vaiśaṃpāyana into the narrative (1.13), a sage of a previous generation who once recited the *Mahābhārata* during the snake sacrifice of Janamejaya. This snake sacrifice has not much relevance to the *Mahābhārata* story, but Vaiśaṃpāyana describes why it took place (1.13-53). From here on until the end of the *Mahābhārata* the Sūta quotes Vaiśaṃpāyana, emerging now and then by name to introduce a new episode. After Vaiśaṃpāyana has related the history of the snake sacrifice that he is attending, he is invited to recite the *Mahābhārata* to King Janamejaya who is a descendant of Arjuna. At this point, the third shell is reached, for Vaiśaṃpāyana, who had heard the story from its composer Vyāsa, quotes him from here on (1.54-18.5.25). So the *Mahābhārata* has three beginnings: namely, Vyāsa's narrative (1.54ff.), Vaiśaṃpāyana's account which is Vyāsa's preceded by the snake episode (1.13ff.); and the third, the Sūta's which is Vaiśaṃpāyana's preceded by a few fables and myths (1.1ff.).

As the narrative unfolds there are very few violations of this frame. Except for a short section of the twelfth book (chs. 327-339), the epic composer has not confounded the levels. It is a formal unit, a unit of staggering proportions but undeniably welded together by a grand design.

This layering of the Epic has given rise to speculation that we have to do with three historically separable stages of development. Traditionally, they are said to form the beginnings of three different works, the *Mahābhārata,* the *Bhārata* and the *Jaya,* respectively.[8] We may also distinguish between the so-called *sauta-* (from *sūta- "bard"*) tradition and the *māntra-* (from *mantra-* "sacred formula") tradition. The former would correspond to the heroic, or at least martial tradition, the other to the body of orthodox Brahmanical doctrines that figure so prominently in the *Mahābhārata.*

The *Mahābhārata's* narrative is not continuous, or simple. Many plots are interwoven as the story proceeds. By the introduction of new speakers at various points, we are often presented with flashbacks showing the reasons why a certain character acts in a certain manner. The main plots can be outlined as follows:

1. The frame story, Janamejaya's snake sacrifice. Janamejaya's anger at the death of his father by a snakebite induces him to perform a snake sacrifice. The snakes deserve this fate because of an event in the mythological past, when they quarreled with Garuḍa's mother, Vinatā. She cursed them that they would perish in a sacrifice.

2. The *Bhārata* story, the Great War. The outline of this story has been presented in the preceding chapter. The battle was essentially a conflict between two branches of one family over a piece of land. This feud developed into a bloody battle, in which one branch, the Kurus, was completely annihilated and the other barely survived. The land, part of the Gangetic plain, with its capital Hāstinapura, became the Pāṇḍavas' patrimony.

The factors leading up to the war have been spun out in great detail. Some hark back to mythological antiquity; others are psychological. The Kurus envied and hated the Pāṇḍu brothers ever since childhood because of their superior physical endowments, and attempted repeatedly to assassinate them. To all this hostility the Pāṇḍus did not react with violence. On the contrary, they invited them to Yudhiṣṭhira's great sacrifice where the Kurus' envy again was aroused. With equanimity the Pāṇḍus accepted the invitation to the gambling match, though fairly well assured of their doom. Only when the Kurus committed the unforgivable offense of mortally insulting an honorably married woman did they bring upon their heads a sin that only blood could erase. For many interpreters of *Mahābhārata,* especially the modern Hindu, this is the cardinal plot of the Epic: a woman was insulted and avenged. Repeatedly afterward Draupadī reminds her often meek husbands of the shame she had undergone at the hands of their enemies. Duḥśāsana's death at Bhīma's hands and the drinking of his blood (8.61) atone for the insult.

On this basic epic plot a superstructure has arisen of narratives to explain and justify the behavior of the various characters. As in other epics, a person's actions are thought of as conditioned by incidents in his past, or even in a former life, such as a curse, a good deed, or a miraculous birth, rather than by his psychological motivation. His character has to be inferred from his activities, and only rarely does the author describe a person's character traits explicitly.

Part of the superstructure consists of genealogies of the heroes, especially as described in chapter 1.62-128. Here we learn how Bhārata was born to Śakuntalā, and in what complicated manner his descendants, the Pāṇḍus and Kurus, are related to each other. The account is as follows: Satyavatī operates a ferry on Yamunā for her father. A sage Parāśara, while being ferried across, falls in love with her and begets the later famous Kṛṣṇa Dvaipāyana Vyāsa, composer of the *Mahābhārata*. Vyāsa does not marry, but acts for the deceased King Vicitravīrya to beget offspring with his widows Ambikā and Ambālikā. They give birth to the blind Dhṛtarāṣṭra and his younger half-brother Pāṇḍu. The latter marries, Kuntī and Pṛthā, but is unable to beget children. Through the intervention of the gods Dharma, Vāyu, and Indra, he becomes the nominal father to Yudhiṣṭhira, Bhīma, and Arjuna; with the aid of the Aśvins Pṛthā gives birth to Sahadeva and Nakula. Dhṛtarāṣṭra's wife, Gāndhārī, brings forth Duryodhana and his ninety-nine brothers and one sister.

This confusing line of descent holds one interesting legal point, namely, who was the legitimate successor to the throne of Hāstinapura. Dhṛtarāṣṭra was older than Pāṇḍu, but could not reign on account of his blindness. Upon Pāṇḍu's death, the throne should have passed to his oldest male offspring, Yudhiṣṭhira, who instead, for a time became a ward of his uncle Dhṛtarāṣṭra.[10] Later on, rather than laying claim to the throne, he withdrew to Indraprastha leaving Duryodhana, his junior (1.107.26), in power as Lord of Hāstinapura.

Another part of the superstructure consists of a justification of this bloody battle in metaphysical terms. To the more refined spirits of later Hinduism, the brute description of feats of heroism without a moral overtone must have been uncomfortable. As a result, the main characters of the battle are invested with another role, that of embodying gods or demons. In a celestial struggle between gods and wicked Asuras, the latter threaten to overcome the forces of good by incarnating themselves on earth. The gods appeal to Brahma who orders them also to assume human form and to continue the battle on earth (1.58). The subsequent identification of the personages in our Epic with *avatāras* of gods, is carried out thoroughly, but is, on the whole, of little interest. Yudhiṣṭhira, Vidura, and Bhīṣma all represent Dharma on earth, and the other Pāṇḍu brothers have already been described. Most Kurus are incarnations of evil demons. Kṛṣṇa represents Nārāyaṇa, on earth (1.61). After the battle is over and the heroes have entered heaven, they are reunited with the gods whose manifestations they were. Having played their cosmic role, the human actors cease to be enemies and so the whole tragic *Mahābhārata* can be terminated in a spirit of harmony and peace.

This latter plot has the virtue that it unites the whole complex of battle stories and moral doctrines under one great plan, that of a cosmic struggle whose outcome is decided on earth by apparently frail human beings. The *Bhagavad-gītā,* proclaimed as it is at the beginning of the critical struggle, effectively lends a metaphysical significance to otherwise reprehensible acts of violence and sets them against a background of a combat between the forces of righteousness and those of lawlessness. The lengthy moral discourses, from this point of view, aim at reinforcing a spirit of right morality that ought to prevail among the listeners in order that the agents of Righteousness will gain the upper hand.[11]

Besides these three principal plots and their superstructures, there are a number of subordinate plots interwoven in the epic story to explain or justify the behavior of the warriors on the battlefield. A few of these are:

1. The mental conflict of Karṇa who knew he was fighting his half-brothers, but hated them and his mother.
2. Ambā's rejection by Bhīṣma and her subsequent rebirth to avenge herself.
3. Droṇa who was insulted by Drupada and later killed by the latter's son.
4. Kṛṣṇa who receives assistance from the Pāṇḍu brothers to kill his enemies Jarāsaṃdha and Śiśupāla and becomes their adviser and Arjuna's charioteer.
5. Arjuna's adventures in Indra's heaven and at Kṛṣṇa's court.

6. The two sacrifices Yudhiṣṭhira undertakes, one a sacrifice of royal consecration and the other the horse sacrifice.

Numerous other incidental stories and episodes exist, all connected with the epic story by a very thin thread indeed.

III *Statistics*

The *Mahābhārata* consists of eighteen books, or *Parvans* of greatly varying lengths.[12] The longest is the *Śānti-parvan* with 12,892 verses, the shortest the *Mahāprasthānika-parvan* with only one hundred and six. Each book is divided into sub-*parvans,* which in turn comprise a variable number of chapters, *adhyāyas*. The sub-*parvans* usually deal with one specific topic, whereas the division into chapters is quite arbitrary. Some chapters are as long as two hundred stanzas (e.g. 13.14), others contain as few as six (e.g. 13.13). *Parvans* and sub-*parvans* have names; chapters do not. The verses are usually two-line stanzas which follow a metrical pattern.

The exact length of the *Mahābhārata* has long been a subject of contention. Of all the four editions of the Epic, each shows a different total number of stanzas. The problem is compounded by the fact that in the introduction (1.2), a detailed enumeration of the contents is given, the so-called *Parvasaṃgraha* which lists the number of stanzas as one hundred thousand. None of the printed editions of the Epic came near that number. When a critical edition was begun in 1929 (see below p. 141), hope was expressed that a conscientious comparison of the various current text versions would ultimately yield this self-professed number of stanzas. When it appeared that there were great differences between the *Parvasaṃgraha* figures and the actual number of stanzas in each book, scholars resorted to arithmetical sleights-of-hand in order to smooth out the discrepancies. But it is quite clear now that the *Parvasaṃgraha* figures cannot be made to agree with those found in our *Mahābhārata.* In the Critical Edition, the total number of stanzas given in the Parvan-index is 95,586, whereas the actual counted number is only about 73,900. It is safe to assume that the compiler of the *Parvan*-index was not too concerned about the accuracy of his count.[13]

The oldest manuscript of the *Mahābhārata* found so far, is only about seven hundred years old. Quotations are known from much earlier works.[14]

IV *Composition*

The *Mahābhārata* is largely composed of stanzas designed to be recited or sung. The prose passages make up an insignificant proportion, less than 1 per cent, of the entire text. The majority of the verses are composed in a meter called *śloka-* "praise," or *anuṣṭubh,* "after-praise." A smaller part belongs to the *triṣṭubh-* "three-praise" class. Sporadically, other classes of meter occur.

Epic stanzas (with the exception of a few *ārya*-stanzas), are classified according to the number of syllables they contain. A *śloka* has sixteen syllables per half-verse, a *triṣṭubh* thirteen. The *śloka* consists of two similar half-verses, each of which can be divided into two dissimilar quarter verses of eight syllables each. A syllable is either heavy or light. Light syllables contain a short vowel followed by at most one consonant. All other syllables are heavy. The succession of light and heavy syllables determines the metrical pattern of the verse: the posterior quarter *śloka* of any verse should have for syllables six-seven-eight, the succession: heavy-light-indifferent, whereas the prior quarter *śloka* has not so rigid a scheme, but allows a few dozen variations. These variations, as well as those of the syllables one to five of the posterior quarter *śloka,* break the monotony of the thousands upon thousands of successive verses. They are usually recited in a particular sing-song manner which varies with the locality in India. The *triṣṭubh* meter has also a free pattern permitting many variations.[15]

The verse meter of both *śloka* and *triṣṭubh* goes back to the ancient *Vedas*. From the very free scheme of *Vedic* verse an evolution can be traced in literary history to a rigidly defined set of metrical patterns found in the post-Gupta literature. The Epic meter lies somewhere between these extremes but it is not homogeneous throughout the Epic. Large parts are found in which the meter is relatively free and not easily classifiable. In other portions, especially the twelfth and thirteenth books, the meter conforms to the theoretical classifications established by later metrists. A knowledge of the history of the meter, therefore, allows us to determine roughly the relative age in which the different portions of the Epic were composed. If we find episodes with large blocks of stereotyped, theoretically perfect meter, we can assume a later date of composition. On the other hand, a simple, artless, "flawed" meter would point to an earlier date. In the absence of clear-cut data for determining the age of any part of the *Mahābhārata,* meter is used as an indication of its antiquity, together with other equally circumstantial evidence.

V *Language*

The *Mahābhārata* is written in Sanskrit, the language that is presumed to have been current in northern India up to approximately the second century B.C. and thereafter as a language of a small portion of India proper. The Sanskrit language is known from literary works which must have originated considerably earlier than the first purely Sanskrit inscription that has come down to us (second century A.D.). The archaic Sanskrit of the *Vedas* differs greatly from that of our text. The Sanskrit language underwent a drastic change between Vedic times (around 1000 B.C.) and the time of Epics and *Purāṇas*. Its evolution has not halted there either, for in later times we find it changed still more in vocabulary, syntax, and morphology, apparently to conform to the speech habits of the speakers of vernacular languages.

Standard, correct Sanskrit was prescribed in the grammar of the grammarian Pāṇini (fourth century B.C.). Epic Sanskrit by comparison is quite grammatical. It is perhaps closer to informal Sanskrit than any other works we possess, but it also contains hundreds of "incorrect" word forms. A few archaic features are preserved, such as the augmentless imperfects (e.g., *vyavaśīryanta* 2.72.22 "they fell down") and aorists (e.g., *bhaiḥ* 1.128.8 "be afraid"), and a great number of aberrant sandhi formations, especially hiatus. The word *tmānam* "self" (acc. sg.) is found frequently instead of the correct *ātmānam*. On the whole, however, Epic Sanskrit is unsophisticated rather than archaic: it tends to simplify and generalize the rules of Sanskrit grammar following the trend that dominates its historical development from ancient times on. There is an increasing use of thematic vowels both in verb and noun stems, where originally root stems were used. Thus we find *dadati, kurvati, hanati* for the root verbs *dadāti* "he gives," *karoti* "he does," *hanti* "he kills"; also nouns like "*kṣudhā-* for *kṣudh-* "thirst," *pāda-* for *pād-* "foot," and so on. Verbal derivatives are formed with a union vowel *-i-* more frequently than was common in Vedic; active and middle endings occur without discrimination of meaning; the feminine of the active present participle is formed freely from either the stem *-atī-,* or *-antī-*; the finite verb endings of the first plural *-mas* and *-ma* are often interchanged; the gerunds frequently appear as *-ya* after simple verb roots, instead of *-tvā,* e.g., *uṣya* "having lived."

The most striking difference found in Epic compared to archaic Sanskrit, however, is in its syntax. Vedic tends to express an action by a finite verb, whereas in Epic Sanskrit the use of the participial construction, both passive and active, increases greatly. Also the impersonal passive construction with the gerundive participle becomes more common. Epic Sanskrit is approximately at the halfpoint mark in the development of the syntax from Vedic to late Sanskrit which abounds in participial constructions. Word composition varies from one part of the Epic to another. Whether the relative scarcity of long compounds compared to, for instance, the poet Bhāsa and the later ornate compositions is a historic feature, or attributable to the simple diction of the Epic, remains to be investigated.[16]

In the Epic language, therefore, we have found another measure with which to gauge the relative date of composition of any one piece of text. The language, like the meter, is not homogeneous.

VI *Style and Character*

Prosodically, the Sanskrit literary style has also undergone an evolution from rather simple, unornamented prose and verse to a very elaborate, contrived poetic diction which we find from about the seventh century A.D. on. As in the case of meter and grammar, the *Mahābhārata* occupies an intermediate position. By far the greater part does not exhibit the artificial poetic niceties so beloved to the classical poets of later time. On the other hand, it is not entirely devoid of them, and a few simple devices, such as alliteration and similar sound effects, are found rather frequently.[17] Recited by a skilled bard, the *Mahābhārata* can catch the attention and fire the imagination of the listener by its vivid imagery and simple, straightforward diction. For instance, when Arjuna tells his charioteer Uttara to advance to meet the enemy, he says:

> O Uttara, the wretch you see with red eyes, clad in a tigerskin, employing a blue standard, standing on his chariot—this is Kṛpa's army of chariots—Take me just to this one. I shall show a swift missile to this tough archer! The one whose standard is a beautiful pot made of gold, he is, indeed, the teacher Droṇa, the best of all arm-bearers. O hero, make a circle around him in his honor, serene in mind, and right here, without contradiction; this is the eternal law. If Droṇa will strike me first in the body, then I shall strike him and he will not be angry (4.50.4-8).

Occasionally, however, we encounter passages which are technically so complex that they would qualify as genuine pieces of ornate poetry. An example is the language of the following piece. The king should act like a peacock:

> He should always keep his counsels concealed, observing silence, like a peacock in the fall; he should be polished and delicate in speech, full of majesty (just as the peacock has a smooth voice and body and is beautiful), experienced in giving commands. He should be cautious at places where misfortune may enter, just as (a peacock is cautious about coming to distress at slippery spots) near waterfalls. He should put his trust in perfected Brahmans, just as (a peacock, shunning muddy waters, trusts himself) to rain, or mountain water. The king desirous of obtaining an object should (like a peacock desirous of an object) maintain a topknot (just as the peacock sets up his crest), as if it were a banner of righteousness. Always should he hold the rod of chastisement uplifted and behave with circumspection (as the peacock lifts up its legs (?) and steps cautiously). And having seen the income and expenditure among the people (he is like the peacock) flying from tree to tree (looking for ripe fruit) (12.120.7-9).

In pieces like the latter, which are attempts at rhetorical elegance full of puns and forced turns of phrase, the emphasis has shifted from an audience-oriented recitation to an exhibition of the cleverness of the composer in manipulating the Sanskrit language. In later literature such skill was appreciated greatly. The *Mahābhārata,* being in the main devoid of these niceties, fails to rate as a great work of literature by the standards of Sanskrit criticism.

Throughout the Epic, we are confronted with a text intended to be recited and listened to, rather than read. It has all the earmarks of an oral composition: it is repetitious, full of clichés and tag verses that the bard has committed to memory. It often contains superfluous words such as vocatives addressed to an audience presumed to be present. Even meaningless particles and interjections are inserted where the metric structure requires it. To a large extent, the text consists of dialogues which are quoted directly. For instance, to introduce the battle report, the sage Vaiśaṃpāyana, having described the array of armies, continues "Dhṛtarāṣṭra spoke: 'On the field of righteousness, the field of Kuru/ My (allies) as well as the Pāṇḍavas / Gathered desirous of battle / What did they do, O Saṃjaya?' Saṃjaya spoke: . . ." Dhṛtarāṣṭra's leading question prompts Saṃjaya to report the whole battle as if he were an eyewitness, often with childish amazement and horror, which contributes much to the liveliness of the battle account.

The battle took place ages ago, in a better era, when people were heroic and capable of feats of incredible fortitude and strength. Heroes dispatch thousands of arrows at one another, the sun is obscured by clouds of arrows and spears, a huge elephant is struck down with one blow of a mace and armies lose thousands upon thousands daily and still remain as powerful as ever. Exaggerated numbers, proportions, and weapon feats all contribute to an unreal atmosphere of heroic grandeur. Metaphoric passages abound. The battlefield is often compared to a river, "a horrible river of bloody current. Its course was deflected by stacks of bones, it was weedy with waterplants which were the warriors' hair; chariots were its pools, arrows its bays, horses its fish; it was hard to approach. It was full of rocks formed by severed heads, abounding with crocodiles which were the elephants, rich in foam which were the coats of mail and headbands, and bows formed its islands, swords its turtles. It was rich in trees which were the banners and standards, and it was eroding its banks that were those who were about to die. It was filled with shoals of ghouls (and) increased the (population of the) country of Yama. Many valiant warriors crossed that river, O king, with boats that were horses, elephants and chariots, relinquishing fear" (6.99.33ff.). We also find the battle compared to a sacrifice (5.139.29-53) whereby Bhīma's drinking of Duḥśāsana's blood is compared to the drinking of soma.

The characterization of the opposing parties and the individual heroes is on the whole fairly consistent. Throughout, the Pāṇḍavas are the injured party; they are at a disadvantage in having a smaller army and in facing a ruthless enemy which is determined to exterminate them. Only at the expense of great energy, deeds of valor, and physical prowess do they emerge victorious from the struggle. The heroes have epithets bespeaking their prowess: Arjuna is called *Vijaya* "victor" and *Dhanaṃjaya* "winner of wealth." One of Bhīma's standard epithets is *Bhīmaparākrama* "he who has a terrible valor." Both are pugnacious warriors, Bhīma perhaps being the more impulsive and reckless of the two, lashing around with his mace and laying low the enemy. Arjuna is more thoughtful and deliberate, shooting arrows where they are likely to have effect. The twins, Nakula and Sahadeva, by their mere actions do not stand out, but remain accessory figures.[18]

Yudhiṣṭhira is rarely depicted as a fighting hero. In a truly heroic spirit, he maintains a noble aloofness from the slights he undergoes at the hands of his adversaries, in their youth as well as later in the gambling hall and in the forest. He seldom deigns to defend himself against insults and calumny, secure as he is in the conviction that Justice, his father, is on his side.

Of the Kuru party, Duryodhana is a wicked, though powerful enemy. Karṇa suffers from a feeling of inferiority, though he is one of the greatest heroes. Truly evil is Duryodhana's uncle Śakuni who has not one single redeeming character trait. The Kurus are torn by internal strife, especially because of Dhṛtarāṣṭra's weakness and ambivalent attitude toward the war.

If the epic and episodic narrations are lively and entertaining, the moral and didactic passages are about as uninspiring as a nineteenth-century fundamentalist sermon. Aside from being repetitious, they are full of obscure phraseology alluding to half-explained (and perhaps half-understood) metaphysical and ethical doctrines. The didactic passages have an authoritative tone that one associates with a teacher-pupil relationship whereby the teacher solemnly proclaims verities which the pupil is expected to absorb uncritically and submissively. For instance: Those who apply themselves to their studies, delight in listening to their elders, are observant of their meditative exercises and their vows, are firm in truth, do not contradict their instructors, are always alert and uncritical of their elders' activities . . . they go to (heaven) (13.105.33f.).

In contrast to the epic tradition of powerful wrestling bouts, gleeful descriptions of the slaughter of enemies and a delight in gory battle scenes, the Brahmanical ideology frowns on revelling in open violence. For the orthodox tradition, non-violence is the highest goal and aggression is repressed and denied. The later redactors of the Epic have, therefore, altered the tone of the *Mahābhārata.* The heroes of the pseudo-epic are Bhīṣma, the epitome of the old man full of wisdom, Kṛṣṇa, the god incarnate, and again, Yudhiṣṭhira, but more fully playing his role as God Justice on earth. For a hero to be acceptable to the Hindu, he has to have the qualities attributed to Yudhiṣṭhira: he has to be self-denying and to suffer beatifically, emerging serene and purified after many adverse experiences. In Yudhiṣṭhira the contrast between the Hindu hero and the Western hero shows clearly, in that the admirable part of his character lies not in what he does, but in his abstention from acts of violence. Even when injustice is being committed and his interference might save the honor or life of another human being, as in the case of Draupadī's disrobement, as a true hero he refuses to act.

VII *The Epic Setting*

In spite of the *Mahābhārata's* magnitude, comparatively little can be learned about the social and economic world in which the action moves. Moreover, much that can be inferred by indirect means is self-contradictory, so that one is easily led to erroneous conclusions if concentrating on a small part of the Epic only. We do not know from objective accounts whether the Great Battle ever took place, nor assuming it was fought, do we know the date. Traditional Hindu chronology regards the war as the end of the previous *Yuga* and Hindu estimates range from 3137 B.C. to the battle of the sixth century B.C. between Cyrus of Persia and the Indians.[19] It is unlikely that the date can ever be settled. Neither extrapolation from genealogical tables, nor astronomical data, nor the attempts to tie it in with historical events, not to mention the magical decipherment of cryptograms in the verses of the *Mahābhārata,* are likely to lead to success.

Geographically, the Epic story takes place in Northern India and a vast area surrounding it. This area stretched from the Greek occupied lands in the west and northwest and from Nepal, and the country of the Chinese, to the northeast where the Assamese and the Vaṅgas, probably Bengal people, were known. Among the people of the south, the names Kaliṅgas, Āndhras, Drāviḍas, Colas, Karṇātakas, Keralas, Koṅkanas, and Madrakas are referred to. Pārsikas "Persians" and even Antioch and Rome were mentioned. Within this vast area, Bhārata land was the chosen place where pious people dwelt: "Dear was our Bhārata land to god Indra and to Father Manu, as to the saints and mighty warriors of old, and dear to all men now is this our Bhārata land" (6.9.5-12). As such, it was not confined to the narrow boundaries that Patañjali assigned to it, i.e., the area east of the Sarasvatī River, south of the Himālayas, west of the Sarayū and north of the Vindhya mountains. Nor is it the same Arya-land that Manu (2.22f.) describes as "the land between the Himālayas and the Vindhya mountains, whereas any country where the black-buck does not roam is fit only for slaves!" Bhārata land was the area where the Aryan institutions were observed.[20]

Kuru country for which the Great Battle was fought, probably lay in the fertile plain between the Ganges and Yamunā rivers. Its capital, the city of Hāstinapura, has not been located. According to legend, it was flooded by the Ganges and has since disappeared.[21] Indraprastha, where the Pāṇḍu brothers settled and which they had to cut out of the jungle, has not been identified at all. Kurukṣetra, the scene of the battle, is said to have been situated in the plains near Delhi. The Indians' lack of historic sense makes it very hard to determine where tradition ends and fiction begins.

A fair amount is known about the institutions and fighting habits of the ruling classes. Here, following Hopkins' *Ruling Caste,*[22] it is expedient to distinguish two different sets of social conditions, those of the battle story and those presented to us by the teachings of the pseudo-epic. The first must be gleaned from stray references throughout the Epic; the second is usually presented as a body of doctrines conceived by the Brahman caste, logically consistent and ethically correct in so far that the Brahmans occupy a position of superiority.

The social atmosphere in which the actual Epic takes place is that of a predominantly rural society. Large ranges and forests are owned by cattle barons, like Virāṭa, who periodically engage in skirmishes with their neighbors. He lives in a rather simple capital city and throughout the territory are scattered villages, hamlets, and hermitages. The people raised cattle and crops. The country was ruled by a king who was not an absolute monarch, but rather a member of the aristocracy who had gained prominence. Yudhiṣṭhira strove to become such a king through his sacrifice of royal consecration. The other noblemen paid tribute to him, and in time of war could be called to take command of the army, or to serve as the king's supporters. The royal house was merely one of several prominent families, the *mahākulas* who constituted the effective government. These noblemen valued physical strength, ate meat, and drank spirituous beverages.

Their battles were fought with little regard for any warriors' code. They used four-horse chariots coached by a charioteer, the warrior standing on the two-wheeled chariot and flinging missiles at his opponents. The usual technique of attack was to shoot the charioteer dead and then to finish the car warrior. The horses too were often killed in order to render the occupants of the chariot helpless. The armor was made of brass, copper, and iron. Bows and arrows were the main weapons, and at close hand warriors fought with swords, maces, axes, and other short weapons. The discus, or rather, throwing ring, was also used. Often two or more warriors would join to slay another one.

About the common people and the slaves we learn very little. A very lowly position is occupied by the Niṣādas. They were fishermen or hunters and could apparently be murdered without scruple. Ekalavya was a Niṣāda (see 1.122) and so were the six persons who perished in the Pāṇḍavas' house of gum.

In these days, the king had a court chaplain, a Brahman, who performed religious ceremonies for him. It does not appear that his position originally was very prominent. He did not enjoy the king's confidence and did not participate in political decisions. Bhīṣma and Droṇa, both warriors, as well as the Sūta Saṃjaya, appear in an advisory capacity much more than the court chaplain. Kṛṣṇa, who is not a Brahman, but a warrior from another country, acts more frequently as the adviser for the Pāṇḍavas than their doting house priest Dhaumya, who had attached himself to them after an urgent plea (1.174). Kings often treated their priests with contempt.

But this situation changed, probably gradually. By becoming teachers to the princes and establishing themselves as hereditary chaplains whom the king was expected to consult in his major decisions, the priests must have sought to attain an intimate relation with the king in order to assert their secular power. They held the monopoly in traditional learning which in India at that time had branched out into uncounted sciences and disciplines. They also wrote the Lawbooks. These lawbooks were probably composed contemporaneous with the bulk of the books of Peace and Instruction of the *Mahābhārata.* And they present an entirely different picture of the Indian social scene than we have gleaned from the Epic story itself.

By the time the *Mahābhārata* had been completed at the hands of Brahmanical scholars, the political stiuation had changed considerably. The free rule of the large landowners had made way for a rigid administration under a despotic monarch and his ministers. Now we read of cities with high, concentric walls topped by watchtowers, of wide moats filled with crocodiles and of the king occupying a splendid palace with pleasure groves, dancing halls, gambling halls, liquor saloons, and stores. The king lived in the luxury of an Oriental potentate, served by courtiers, reclining on a soft couch and lulled by celestial music played by beautiful maidens. Brahmans by this time had made great progress in the theory of statehood and were experts at classifying and systematizing their environment. They used their learning to promote the image of the priest as an awe-inspiring person endowed with magic powers. "Neglect kills cattle, O king, but one single priest when angered, slays a realm" (5.40.7).

We learn most about the caste system from the priestly discourses. It is quite conceivable that the classification of society into four *varṇas* "colors," was entirely their invention. The priests stand at the pinnacle of creation. All creation is subordinate to them (5.61-3), and they lay down prescriptions as to how they may be placated. Their duty is to perform sacrifices which serve to perpetuate the world order. For these acts they are to be rewarded liberally by the king.

The second caste, the warriors, knights, kings and other rulers, have the simple duties of ruling justly, fighting heroically, and being generous to Brahmans. The king should be righteous and just; he should not slay children, old men, anyone who is running away, anyone who holds a straw in his mouth, or anyone who has surrendered in battle (12.118.22-26; 12.286). The earth is the king's wife (12.239.50 and *passim*). The ideal of statehood is a harmonious symbiosis of king and priest by which the world is supported.

The other two castes are the Vaiśyas and Śūdras. The former probably represent the greater part of the uneducated citizenry, the people of the country, whereas the Śūdras were their slaves. The priestly theoreticians assign the task of tilling the soil and trade and commerce to the Vaiśyas; the Śūdras who are self-indulgent and do not study Vedas (12.182) serve the other castes. But even Śūdras should not undertake lowly occupations like acting and leatherwork (12.283). Elsewhere in the *Mahābhārata* the Śūdras are a warrior tribe[23] (7.6.6).

In practice, the caste distinction may not have been observed so rigorously. We read elsewhere (12.181.15) that all castes originally were Brahmans; the apostate through cupidity became the other castes. Caste is inherited, but here and there a vertical movement in the system is recognized. "A Śūdra by a righteous disposition may become a Vaiśya, even a Kṣatriya, yea, even a Brahman" (3.203.11-12). Karṇa is raised from a position of charioteer to that of a king without much protest from the other warriors (1.126). The Pāṇḍu brothers do not hesitate to assume lowly occupations at Virāṭa's palace. Similarly, one's behavior can downgrade one from a high to a low position (3.206.11). Under stress a Brahman may perform the work of a Kṣatriya and Vaiśya, though never that of a Śūdra (12.282-83). Other caste duties are described in this same chapter. The Kṣatriyas' martial duty is proclaimed vociferously by Kuntī (5.130) and again by Vidurā (5.131-35).

CHAPTER 4

Beliefs and the Sectarian Faiths

MORAL and religious precepts in the *Mahābhārata,* as it is interpreted by the Indian people of today, reflect the Hindu culture of the educated upper classes. This culture can be termed the "Great Tradition." It is and has been the patrimony of a relatively small group of educated, sophisticated Hindu courtiers and intellectuals who find their own metaphysical notions about the purpose of life and its relation to afterlife, death, and rebirth reflected in the Epic. This great tradition has been most influential in establishing Hindu culture over the vast area it now occupies. Most Hindus, both poor and wealthy, lower and upper class, will be at least familiar with the concepts of *saṃsāra-* "cycle of rebirths" and *karman-* "action" and its retribution in a following life. These particular concepts are as widespread and generally accepted as is the concept of deity.[1] Many will believe them to be true, even if they do not believe anything else.

However, numerous local popular beliefs exist, which are often contradictory to the doctrines of the Epic.[2] Such popular beliefs also occur in the *Mahābhārata* and are often set down with naïve impartiality cheek by jowl with doctrines of esoteric profundity. We find beliefs in monsters, spirits, and ogres that roam in the night and abduct children. The spirits of the departed (*pretas*) haunt the battlefields shrieking like dying soldiers and keeping company with ghosts. They remain in this unhappy state until the surviving relatives have performed the proper rites, whereupon the spirits pass on to the realm of the *Pitṛs* "fathers." There are different classes of *pitṛs*. They are associated with different phases of the moon, and in the hereafter are dependent for their welfare on the liberality of their descendants. A father is saved by a son from going to a hell called *put* (12.20.14), so that only those who have sons can go to heaven. Every Hindu feels enjoined to perform ceremonies for his departed forefathers and to beget male offspring so that he in turn may count on sustenance during his lunar sojourn.

Among the terrifying monsters of the Epic, we find the *Bhūtas,* the *Rākṣasas* and the *Piśācas.* They stalk at night, disturb the sacrifices of pious Brahmans, and feast on the corpses of fallen soldiers. All are considered to be malicious and noxious, though Rākṣasas are perhaps a trifle more human than the other two groups. They are also mortal. Bhīma marries a Rākṣasī (1.143), and another Rākṣasī becomes tutelary goddess to King Jarāsaṃdha's father (2.16). The Piśācas were probably originally a tribe of cannibals living in northwest India. Higher in the scale of spirits stand the *Yakṣas* and *Gandharvas.* The former are originally spirits of trees and of bodies of water that are locally deified and later became identified with a class of gods of the Great Tradition. A Yakṣa has "monstrous eyes, a great body, is as high as a palm tree, resembling the blazing sun, irresistible, looking like a mountain" (3.287.20). Often they are benevolent and together with the Gandharvas form the retinue of the God of Wealth, Kubera. Female Yakṣiṇīs are also known and are said to be beautiful women similar to the *Apsarases,* or heavenly nymphs. On two occasions Gandharvas delivered battle against human beings and were barely defeated. Only the Pāṇḍavas' great might could overwhelm them. The Apsarases are forever youthful nymphs who are often employed by the gods Indra and Śiva to seduce some mortal who aspires to too much spiritual power: Śakuntalā's mother was an Apsaras.

Rarely, in the Epic, do we hear of individual monsters or demigods; usually they are referred to as a class participating in one event or another. As a result, their physical traits are scarcely ever depicted in detail.

Besides the belief in spirits, we find that animals, birds, and especially snakes are endowed with a sentient mind. Among the mammals, the ape Hanūman acts as a wise advisor to Bhīma; an ape is also the totem animal sitting on Arjuna's flagstaff. The cow, even in the present day, is a sacred animal to the Hindu. In the Epic we still find references to cows being slaughtered by the thousands in sacrifices, after which they were presumably eaten, but the stern voice of the priest is raised against this practice (12.260.19ff.). In one episode, a cow is said to complain about the wanton carnage committed on her relatives. The mythical wonder cow, Nandinī, realizes all one's wishes. Bull's dung and urine were consumed by a Brahman's apprentice, Uttaṅka, in order to secure Indra's favor (1.3.105).

Elephants function as the mythological guardians of the quarters of the compass. The chief ones are Airāvata, (Indra's elephant), Vāmana, Kumuda, and Añjana (5.97.15). Birds are used for reading omens. Lists are given of auspicious birds, e.g., peacocks, geese, and of those that portend disaster, e.g., hawks, owls, pigeons, and red-footed birds. The most renowned fabulous bird is the Garuḍa, Viṣṇu's mount, a bird of gigantic portions who is the archenemy of the snakes.

Snakes occupy a special place in the *Mahābhārata*.[3] The specific occasion for its recitation was a snake sacrifice (see p. 52) and all through the Epic are scattered remarks reminiscent of a snake cult. Snakes live underground in large worlds of their own, in caves and in deep waters. Some are entirely animal, others semihuman. They are poisonous and fearsome and yet many *Nāgas* "snakes" are mentioned by name and play parts in the Epic, fighting on the side of the Pāṇḍus. The earth is supported by the mythical serpent Śeṣa (5.103.2), and he is later identified with Kṛṣṇa-Viṣṇu. Another snake, Vāsuki, is used as a twirling cord during the churning of the ocean (1.16).

Often geographical locations are declared holy. The Epic is full of references to sacred rivers, lakes, and other bodies of water. Besides the River Ganges, which is the most sacred of all, more than a dozen watering places visited by the Pāṇḍus as they traveled around (3.79-153), lay claim to holiness. Usually they have been sanctified as a result of the exploits of heroes of old. Rivers are sometimes personified: Bhīṣma is Gaṅgā's son and the girl Ambā spent part of her tragic life in a form, half-river, half-human (5.187). Mount Kailāsa is the abode of Śiva and a place where gods assemble. Trees are frequently the object of veneration and are said to be capable of hearing, sight, movement, and feeling (12.177.10ff.). They are inhabited by spirits who require appeasement. One tree, the *Kalāmra,* yields milk, food, clothing and bestows immortality (6.8.13ff.).

Magical practices are referred to, especially in the stories associated with the various *tīrthas* "watering places."[4] For instance, by eating at Maṇināga one will never thereafter be poisoned by snake-bites (3.82.91); by bathing in several different places, one regains one's youth, acquires beauty and fortune (e.g., 3.80.61). The evil eye (*ghoradṛṣṭi-, dṛṣṭaviṣa-* 5.16.26.32) is also referred to. Bull's urine is so potent that by smelling it a barren woman may conceive (4.3.10). Ekalavya made an image of Bhīma and worshipped it, since he could not approach the master (1.123.12f.). A curse is often found as the crux of a plot: Uttañka and Pauṣya exchange curses (1.3.126), Pāṇḍu cannot beget children, because an *ṛṣi* in the form of a deer, mortally wounded by his arrow, curses him that he should die, should he attempt to embrace a woman (1.109.18ff.); Kahoda curses his unborn child that it should be born crooked (3.132). Such stories are very common.

All these incidentals in the Epic story throw into relief the frame of reference and the value system of Epic man. His lack of concern for discriminating between the rational and the irrational is noteworthy.

The epic gods are to a large extent inherited from the *Vedas,* at least in name. The Vedic gods originated as personifications of atmospheric and elemental phenomena and were hymned and praised with great eloquence and devotion. As such, the gods are intimately associated with the Great Tradition, whose protagonists, the ubiquitous priests, made a practice of memorizing the *Vedas*. In the Epic, their importance is reduced considerably, but on the other hand, their numbers are augmented by hosts of new gods. The number of gods in the *Mahābhārata* is difficult to estimate. One need not attach much importance to such astronomical figures as 33,000, or 88,000 that are sometimes quoted. The gods proper (*Devas*) have as their archenemies the *Asuras,* powerful, evil anti-gods. In their continuous battles with the Devas they usually lose. Among the Devas, the most renowned are Indra, the Lord of the Gods, also the god of thunder and in a way the patron god of the Pāṇḍus; Agni, the god of fire; Sūrya, the Sungod, best known as Karṇa's father; Varuṇa, the god of water and the blue expanse of heaven; Vāyu, the impetuous, powerful wind god and the Maruts his stormy associates; and finally, the Aśvins, heavenly physicians. All these are prominent Vedic gods. The Epic also knows Yama, the god of death who ties the soul of a mortal in a noose and takes it South; Skanda, the war-god, and Śiva, an ascetic god. Soma who in the Veda was the deified sacrificial drink, has become in the Epic the male god of the moon. On Viṣṇu see Chapter 5.

To laud the gods was one important purpose of the Vedic chants, and in the Epic we still find nominal homage paid to them. For example, there is a hymn to Agni (5.16.1-8) and to Indra (5.16.13-18) to the Aśvins (1.3.60-70), but also a hymn to the Nāgas (1.3.139-146), quite unorthodox, indeed. Most often, gods are depicted as having limited powers only. Determined Brahmans and ascetics can bend them to their will. They quarrel among each other. Indra's mighty feat of slaying the demon Vṛtra, celebrated in many Vedic hymns, here becomes a tale in which Indra, after his treacherous murder of Vṛtra, here a Brahman, flees from the world in panic at having slain a Brahman (5.9-18). Aside from their nominal provinces of thunder, water, fire, and the like, the gods do not possess marked individual characteristics. They are, on the whole, colorless background figures whose relationship with the human race is one of indifference, unless some threat occurs, or the need for cooperation presents itself. Mighty ascetics sometimes force the gods to yield to their demands, but gods and human beings lead parallel existences. Only when Arjuna requires special weapons, does he appeal to Indra and is then required to fight Śiva to be worthy of them; only when Agni requires assistance in burning down the Khāṇḍava forests, does he request Arjuna and Kṛṣṇa to help him. Sacrifices to the gods increase them (5.16.8), but rarely does a Vedic sacrifice play a crucial role, the way a Brahman's curse does. Yudhiṣṭhira performs two great sacrifices, the *Rājasūya* (2.30-32) and the *Āśvamedha,* or horse sacrifice (14.72-96). The former entitles him to call himself a universal monarch, but a simple game of dice robs him of his royal dignity. When Nala is faced with the gods' inopportune request to act as a middleman, he does not try to dissuade them by sacrifices or acts of devotion, but it is Damayantī's oath of truth which sways them. Incidentally, here we learn how gods differ from mortals: they do not blink their eyes, they do not touch the ground, they do not sweat, and their limbs and garments remain free from dust (3.54.23f.). In the *Ādi-parvan* at least, Śiva, Viṣṇu, and Sūrya have two arms and one face only.[5]

Gods are also identified with the points of the compass, in fact, they are regarded as *lokapālas* "guardians of the quarter" more commonly than as elemental gods. Soma, the moon, governs the North, Indra the East, Yama the South, and Varuṇa the West. Each of these gods, as well as Brahma, has a magnificent palace where he lives in state with hosts of attendants. Indra's palace is in his own heaven, the ultimate meeting place of all heroes who have died in battle. They are entertained by beautiful damsels (12.118.20f.). But those who have acted cowardly in battle will go to one of the many hells that Epic man visualized to exist in the hereafter. The exact number of hells is never stated, but they are referred to in the plural. In one place it is declared that compared to heaven all other places are hell (12.191). The God of Death, Yama, reigns over an abode to which all creatures go who die, except when exempted by some particularly virtuous or courageous deed. Yama does good to the good, bad to the evil ones

(5.42.6). The Pāṇḍu brothers, needless to say, do not go there, nor any of the other warriors of Kurukṣetra, nor do those people who have been generous to priests. Yama's own palace is splendid and luxurious, but some hells are unpleasant: sinners are roasted by fire (3.128.12) or tortured by "forests of swords, hot sands, thorny trees," until they are partially purified and fit to regain birth as worms (13.112). In other, presumably later passages, atonement for evil deeds is more often transferred to the next life.

Under the earth are other worlds, seven, according to one account. One is Pātāla, the watery domain of the snakes, another Rasatāla where living is pleasant.

The *ṛṣis* and *maharṣis* form other classes of superior beings each of whom usually number seven. They are semidivine, immortal sages with great, benevolent powers. Among the divine sages (*devarṣis*), Nārada is frequently mentioned as a messenger from the gods to men.

The gods in the Epic story who function prominently in the plot are not depicted with as much reverence and devotion as are the gods who later became objects of worship in the sectarian faiths, i.e., Viṣṇu, Kṛṣṇa, Nārāyaṇa, and Śiva. Gods like Indra, Agni and Soma may be patronizingly spoken of as mighty and splendid and capable of many deeds of mystery, but when the world of Nārāyaṇa is described (12.322), or the glory of Kṛṣṇa in the *Bhagavad-gītā,* or the power of Viṣṇu is compared to other gods; then we sense the awe with which the author regards the Supreme Being:

> Thou art the purifier of purifiers, the goal of the goal-seekers, O greatest one, the fiercest energy of energies, the highest austerity of austerities. O thou who art revered by him who is beneficent to all (Viṣṇu), by Hiraṇyākṣa and Indra, O giver of great prosperity, O lord, very true one, homage to thee! (13.16.13-14).

In these words, the God Śiva is addressed by one of his devotees.

Modern Hindus are apt to present the higher gods, Viṣṇu, Brahma and Śiva as a *trimūrti-* "trinity" of creator, maintainer, and destroyer, respectively. In the *Mahābhārata,* at least, there is no trace of this belief. "The union of the three highest gods into a trinity forms no part of epic belief. The aim of the later poets is to equalize Kṛṣṇa-Viṣṇu and Śiva as two aspects of God, rather than to establish a trinity. . ."[6] 2Brahma, Viṣṇu, Śiva, and Nārāyaṇa are the true Supreme Beings in the Epic. Their respective devotees claim absolute supremacy for the god they worship. The existence of these different claims has led investigators to assign different authorship to the various devotional passages. According to one theory, the supreme god of the Epic proper was Brahma, or Prajāpati. Later the story was reworked by Viṣṇu worshippers and finally by devotees of Śiva. Such theories, however, are tentative.

Brahma, or Prajāpati "Lord of Creation," was of old the creator and ancestor of the other gods, and of the universe. In three, probably spurious places, he is said to have four faces (12.326.47; 330.56; 338.11). He is also all-knowing and immeasurably wise, the most venerable of gods. Born from a primordial egg that he created himself, he is called *svayaṃbhu-* "the self-created." With dignity he states: "I am Brahma, Lord of creatures, a greater being than I is not found" (3.185.48). He is also the god who decreed the destruction of all creatures (3.168.21) and was about to reduce the world's excessive population increase by means of scorching earth and heaven with the fire of his wrath (12.248.12ff.), but instead was persuaded to introduce Death among living beings. He never gained the popularity of Viṣṇu and Śiva, but remained a venerable arbiter to whom the gods on occasion appealed for counsel or judgment in their disputes.

Śiva, the second important god, has no formal Vedic ancestry. His name literally means "auspicious one," a name presumably designed to palliate his awesome qualities. His appearance is fearful: a hundred tongues, a thousand feet, a pot-belly and ears like arrow heads (13.17). Like Brahma, he has four faces which grew on him when he attempted to remain immobile while a beautiful damsel, Tilottamā, trotted around him (1.203.23ff.). He is also the stern lord of the mountains who practices austerities for many years. His wife is Umā, or Pārvatī "the mountain girl," often identified with the ambivalent mother-goddess Durgā. She pined for Śiva, for many years, until he married her. Another member of the Śiva "family" is the god Skanda, the war-god, whereas Gaṇeśa, the elephant-headed god, does not appear in the *Mahābhārata.*

Śiva gave Arjuna the magic Pāśupata weapon, after having struggled with him for the possession of a slain boar. He received the Ganges on the locks of his head when it fell from heaven (5.109.6) and promised Ambā that she would become a man in her next life. Śiva's most important present-day attribute, the *liñga-,* is only incidentally refered to in the didactic parts of the Epic where his praise is sung (13.17.74; 7.172.86-7). His act of swallowing the world poison is not found in our *Mahābhārata,* but is a Purāṇic story.

The god Viṣṇu is to all intents and purposes the principal god of the *Mahābhārata.* He has Vedic antecedents, but is not very prominent there. As a mythological god, he is closely associated with the sun and its manifestations of brilliance, heat, and fire. His epithets bear that out: "yellow-haired one, thousand-rayed one, courser through heavens," etc. Three steps, from sunrise to apex to sunset, take him through heaven. In their effort to present him as the Supreme Being, the redactors of the Epic have endowed him with the same or even greater power than Indra (7.13.43). He becomes the champion of the gods, a slayer of demons and helps Indra fix his missile to slay Vṛtra (5.10.10).

In later times, Viṣṇu's worship is associated with the belief in his *avatāras,* "descents," from his heavenly abodes to earth, in order to assume the physical body of a mortal, be it animal or human. In this form, Viṣṇu is incarnated at a time of crisis in human history. He then saves the earth by his supernatural powers from destruction at the hands of demoniacal powers. The assignment of *avatāras* to a god and their description, is one of the topics of the *Purāṇas,* works which are chronologically later than the *Mahābhārata.* But already in our Epic we find sundry references to the belief in *avatāras.* Traditionally, ten *avatāras* are recognized, the Fish, the Tortoise, the Boar, the Man-Lion, the Dwarf, Rāma son of Jamadagni, Rāma son of Daśaratha, Kṛṣṇa, the Buddha and the future incarnation of Kalki. The *Mahābhārata* accords the honor of saving mankind from the flood not to Viṣṇu as a Fish, but to Brahma (3.185.48). For the remainder, it is only in the twelfth book, in the passage which is probably spurious (see p. 46) that we find passing references to some of these incarnations, e.g., man-lion, boar, Rāma Jāmadagneya, Rāma Dāśaratha (12.326.73-78; 333.11), but included also are *avatāras* as a goose (12.326.94) and as a horse's head roaming the waters of the ocean.

The *Mahābhārata* story can be read without awareness of the *avatāra* concept. However, the setting of the bloody struggle has presented the devout author with an unmatched opportunity to reinterpret it as the climax of a divine struggle which was decided on earth. Kṛṣṇa in the *Bhagavad-gītā* asserts: "Whenever righteousness becomes lax, O Arjuna, and injustice arises, then I send myself forth to protect the good and bring the evil-doers to destruction; for the secure establishment of the law, I come into being age after age" (*Bhag.* 4.8). Elsewhere we find Kṛṣṇa as an incarnation of Nārāyaṇa in the *Harivaṃśa,* which in this sense is a Purāṇic afterthought with regard to the *Mahābhārata.* But it is justifiable to conclude that at the time the *Mahābhārata* was approaching its final form—and we should remember that we are dealing with a work that developed over some five or six centuries—the *avatāra* of God Viṣṇu had not received the widespread acceptance of later times.[7]

Summarizing we can only conclude that there is not one single mythological system applicable to the whole of the *Mahābhārata.* We find belief in omens, both evil and auspicious, in tree-gods, water nymphs, gods of the quarters, as well as minor god-heads, local deities, and evil spirits that haunt the battlefield. Besides, we have the Great Tradition with the gods of Vedic times: Indra, Varuṇa, Yama, and the Ṛṣis. Finally, the sectarian faiths confined to the worship of one highest god, be it Viṣṇu Nārāyaṇa, Kṛṣṇa, Śiva, or Prajāpati, form the link to the development of faiths in later Hindu times.

Ritual. The ritual for worshipping gods plays a great role in Hinduism, and we find stray references to it in the Epic. Vedic gods are worshipped with sacrifices which are often animals; horses, cows, and smaller domestic animals (3.251.11-12). Besides, they may occasionally be placated by an eloquent eulogy. Common spirits of trees, mountains, and the like are offered flowers, fruit, milk and boiled rice. The spirits of the departed fathers receive balls of boiled rice. Flesh-eating demons naturally have some meat added to their offerings, as well as spirtuous liquor. But in passages of the twelfth and thirteenth book the propriety of animal sacrifice is called into question. The dialogue of the Ṛṣis and gods on whether or not animals are to be slaughtered for the gods (12.324) may well reflect a conflict of the time. Both positive (12.260) and negative (12.249) opinions are expressed.

References to human sacrifices are rare. King Jarāsaṃdha had undertaken a sacrifice to Maheśvara (Śiva) consisting of one hundred rulers (2.13). In another episode, King Somaka murdered his own son Jantu in the belief that he would obtain more offspring (3.127). The warrior's act of sacrifice is the killing of enemies on the battlefield (12.22). This is not merely a manner of speaking, for warriors often announce in the heat of battle that they will send the opposite party to Yama's heaven.

CHAPTER 5

Philosophy and Morality

THE distinction between philosophy, ethics, and religion in Western thinking is not recognized as such in the Indian epic. Rather, its outlook on life can be understood only if the realms of interest governed by these three disciplines are merged into one continuum, a complex set of ideas. The Hindu will dissect it along lines different from those of the West. Epic man is concerned with the notion of *dharma* "duty," a many-faceted concept referring to man's relationship with his environment in terms of a set of obligations and privileges that are inherited when he is born into a particular station in life. One person's *dharma* may be another's sin, because a "human being" as an individualized entity, is insignificant. A human being exists as a creature, a mortal, a biological abstraction, but his role in society is defined by his membership in a particular caste. The one ideal that all human beings share is the quest for righteousness, possessions, and love (*dharma, artha, kāma*). A Kṣatriya's (warrior's) duty, for instance, is to fight and rule. A Brahman, as part of his duty, will try to live according to the four stages of life (*āśramas*), i.e., student, householder, forest recluse, and wanderer. The metaphysical abstractions that we term "philosophy" are speculated on during the third stage of life. Then the Brahman, ripe in years, repairs to a simple hut in the forest to meditate upon the way to attain salvation. So the search for transcendental knowledge for its own sake, which we are apt to associate with the word "philosophy," is not important: in Indian philosophy the emphasis lies on attaining salvation; it is a goal-oriented philosophy.

Indian philosophy developed over a long period of time. It had its beginnings in the *Vedas* and its ancillary works, where it often appears as an unsystematic set of speculations. Nothing in Indian literature ever remains unsystematized for very long, so that by the sixth or seventh century, we find a tidy classification of Hindu philosophy into six systems, the *Nyāya, Vaiśeṣika, Sāṃkhya, Yoga, Advaita Vedānta,* and *Viśiṣṭādvaita Vedānta.* In addition, the non-Hindu sects of Buddhists, Jains, Tāntrists, and others had devised their own metaphysics of salvation.

The *Mahābhārata* was composed at a time when these systems had not achieved the canonization accorded to them by later works. The doctrines of the Veda, however, are often referred to. Time and again, it is asserted that the *Vedas* did not teach enough. They teach that salvation can be achieved through acts of sacrifice, whereas the *Mahābhārata* emphasizes that there is an alternate way, see, for instance, in the *Śānti-parvan,* 260-61, the dialogue between the cow and Kapila. The two doctrines are often contrasted as *pravṛtti-* "activity," or salvation by acts of sacrifice, as opposed to *nivṛtti-* "abstention," the theory of non-action (12.327).

The dominant philosophical trend in the Epic is the *Sāṃkhya.* To characterize it briefly, one can say that it seeks to establish categories which define the origin and composition of the universe and of humanity. It is an early, confused presentation of the *Sāṃkhya;* many of the categories are ill-defined, their relationships nebulous, their nomenclature inconsistent. Even so, they are unmistakingly attempts to understand the structure of the universe, so that with the aid of a proper understanding, one could seek a method of releasing oneself from the shackles of the material world.

On the whole, two concepts underlie all *Mahābhārata* thinking. One is the belief that the human soul is tied to earthly existence by fetters which through great effort may be broken. The soul is then said to be released. If not released, the soul is reborn shortly after death in another body. Its welfare in the next life, in terms of physical comfort and social prestige, are dependent on the net balance of actions, good and evil, performed during some previous existence. Through the operation of an abstract mechanism called *karma,* "action," [1] an automatic account is kept of the ethical quality of the actions performed during one's lifetime. *Karma* is a notion like fate, intangible, invisible, something that is to be accepted and believed. The process of death and rebirth is called *saṃsāra-* "passing through." [2]

The notions of "human soul," "bonds," and "liberation" are universally recognized in the Hindu systems of philosophy, but their definitions vary with the systems. The latter purport to define the nature of the soul and its relation to the other metaphysical entities in a very detailed and logically coherent manner. One philosophical system differs from another in the manner of definition, in the degree of subtlety and sophistication in which obstacles to salvation are erected and overcome, and in the comparative ease with which salvation may be attained. Salvation is usually called *mokṣa* "release, undoing (of a knot)," but the Buddhist term *nirvāṇa* "extinction" is also used.

A second underlying assumption in the *Mahābhārata* is the notion that a person gains in power and esteem if he undergoes hardship. Hardship is understood in several different ways. It may be simply the expenditure of large amounts of wealth, such as in Yudhiṣṭhira's sacrifices, or it may be literally a subjection of oneself to physical discomfort. The Epic sacrifices have rightly been compared to the potlatch ceremonies known from elsewhere in the world (Held, 1935, p. 244). They derive from Vedic ceremonies whereby the sacrificer followed a set of prescribed rules to achieve a certain purpose: to celebrate an important event, or simply to maintain the order of the universe, *ṛta*. The actual oblation was usually a small amount of butter, milk, or dough; sometimes it was an animal. These were burned for the consumption of the gods who were presumed to grant the sacrificer's wishes. From this simple act we can trace a development of increasing emphasis on the minute observation of sacrificial details and a corresponding emergence of the sacrificial priest as an indispensable intermediary between the sacrificer and the gods. The composers responsible for the final redaction of the Epic were priests, and they garnered it with admonitions to perform sacrifices and be liberal to the officiants.[3] Moreover, they inserted many didactic anecdotes showing how profitable it is to favor priests and, contrariwise, what dire fate overtakes the person who offends them.

The Epic also recognizes a form of self-sacrifice whereby a person voluntarily undergoes hardships for a protracted period of time in order to attain a particular end. By his penance he gains power and this power when great enough, will coerce a god into obeying him. An Epic character may deliberately use this device to obtain a child, as Sāvitrī's father did, or to obtain divine weapons, as was Arjuna's aim, or to accomplish other supernatural feats. The notion may go back to a non-Hindu ascetic tradition.[4]

Therefore, many of the episodes and anecdotes of the *Mahābhārata* hinge upon the unquestioning acceptance of the theory of *saṃsāra,* "rebirth," the value of accidental or self-inflicted hardship and the advisability of being liberal to Brahmans. "A man is bound to retrieve that action, be it good or bad, that he is doing" (3.200.5). Śakuntalā blames a previous life for her rejection by Duḥṣanta (1.68.70). Draupadī on one occasion attributes her misfortune to past wrongdoings (4.19.28). Heaven, in this theory, is the abode of the performers of pious actions (*puṇyakṛt-*) whence one returns after the accumulated merit has expired (3.191.2; 247.38-41). Occasionally, God Dharma who is in charge of the karmic law, makes a mistake, as in the case of the *ṛṣi* Māṇḍavya, who was undeservedly treated as a sinner in his next life (1.108). Yudhiṣṭhira at one point even questions the validity of the law of *karma:* "Whether there be a fruit or not of good and evil actions . . . those are the secrets of the gods" (3.32.33). Ambā deliberately tortures herself to force God Śiva to grant her revenge in her next life. The Brahman influence shows in the notion that sin can be erased if one visits certain holy places, e.g., Lake Puṣkara (3.80.45), or listens to the *Mahābhārata.*[5] The otherwise inexpiable sin of killing a Brahman is relieved from Indra after he has performed a horse sacrifice (5.13.12.18).

Less immediately evident in Epic philosophy are the exact physical and metaphysical composition of the universe and the human being, and the exact manner in which release is to be attained. The most eloquent pronouncement on the method of release is the *Bhagavad-gītā-* "Song of the Exalted One." It is often excerpted from the *Mahābhārata* and has become a book of deep religious significance to the Hindu. More than any other part of the Epic, it has gained a status comparable to the Holy Bible in our society. Moreover, it has had an uncommon appeal to the Westerner. No Sanskrit work has been translated so extensively and into so many languages.

The *Bhagavad-gītā* is found as chapters 23-40 of the *Bhīṣma-parvan*. In the Critical Edition, which differs but little from the Vulgate, it has seven hundred stanzas. Western scholars have often doubted whether the *Gītā* is an integral part of the *Mahābhārata,* or whether it is a later interpolation. It is very difficult to decide this issue on any objective basis. We know that the text existed in the eighth century of our era, or about three hundred years after the date we believe the Epic was completed. It is a dialogue between the despondent Arjuna and his charioteer Kṛṣṇa. The arguments Kṛṣṇa uses to induce Arjuna to take up arms, vary greatly in tone. On the one hand we have passages conforming to the heroic setting of the dialogue, e.g., "Either you are slain, or else, victorious, you will enjoy the earth" (6.24.37). Also he attempts to shame Arjuna into resuming the battle "otherwise people will speak of your eternal disgrace" (24.34). On the other hand, some of the arguments are entirely on the metaphysical level and are more consonant with the disquisitions on morality and salvation that form part of the pseudo-epic.

It is not difficult to understand the fascination of the *Bhagavadgītā*. The poetic phraseology, the hypnotic, haunting repetition of words suggestive of a hidden truth, of a higher reality inaccessible to the ordinary human being, all these contribute to an extraordinary effect of tension. We are apt to sympathize with Arjuna, as his conflict is a universal and immediate one: should we do our duty even if it means destroying those who are by affections, custom, and law close to us? Should Arjuna incur the burden of parricide and wholesale bloodshed to acquire what is lawfully his? Is killing, for any reason at all, justified? Does the end justify the means? The solution of the problem is unexpected: Arjuna gradually is made aware that his comprehension of the world is limited, that viewed in another light, seemingly perturbing events lose their fearsomeness. From the perspective of eternity his anxieties are insignificant. Kṛṣṇa raises him to a state in which he is ready to undergo a mystic experience. He becomes ecstatic, awed by his visions, and finally he jubilantly exclaims that his doubts have perished. The reader has passed with him through a catharsis which is almost unique in Indian literature. Few Sanskrit poems are so well worded, so elegantly composed.[6]

The doctrines that Kṛṣṇa propounds in his speech are not logically consistent. Some passages refer to him as a personal god; elsewhere he is one of two spirits, an imperishable and a perishable; in other places he is said to be immanent in the whole universe. In yet others not Kṛṣṇa, but an entity called *brahman* is said to be the only and highest principle of the universe. It has been suggested by an eminent scholar of the *Gītā* that it offered a simplified religious handbook to people who were unable to grasp the subtleties of the post-Vedic philosophical treaties on *mokṣa*. In order to make the abstruse path leading to *mokṣa* more accessible to the populace, the impersonal, absolute principle *brahman* was subordinated to the personified God Kṛṣṇa. We can agree with the same scholar that ". . . the Gītā makes no attempt to be logical or systematic in its philosophy. It is frankly mystical and emotional." [7] The efforts at popularization have certainly met with success.

Next some of the philosophical and didactic disquisitions will be examined which are scattered all over the *Mahābhārata,* sometimes in dialogues, sometimes as sermons. The twelfth book, the Book of Peace, is entirely devoted to them. We shall confine ourselves to short extracts from the *Rājadharma,* the *Āpaddharma,* and the *Mokṣadharma.*

I *On the Morality of Kings*

Yudhiṣṭhira asks Bhīṣma about the duty of a king. What is the most essential thing for a state? Bhīṣma replies:

> The appointment of a king is the most essential thing for a country. A state without a ruler becomes weak and overruled by robbers. In countries without a king, law does not become established. And the people devour each other. In every way anarchy is deplorable. The sacred script states that when one elects a king, one elects Indra. One who desires prosperity should worship the king, just as if he were Indra. One would not live in countries without kings, states the Veda. . . But if a very powerful king should undertake, for the sake of his dominion, to turn to kingless countries, or else, countries whose king has been slain, he should be met and welcomed and worshipped; this is good policy in this matter, for nothing is worse than evil anarchy. If he is treated kindly, all will be well, for a powerful one when angered might even bring about extermination (of his opposition). A great deal of pain suffers the cow that is hard to milk, but one does not hurt the cow that milks well. The wood that bends without being heated, that one does not scorch, but that which does not bend by itself, that is forced to bend. Guided by this parable the wise man should bow before a stronger one. He who bows before a stronger one, he worships Indra. Therefore, a king should always be appointed by one who desires prosperity. No enjoyment of wealth, no enjoyment of wives exist for those who have no ruler (12.67.2-12).
>
> If there were no king in the world, meting out punishment on the earth, the stronger would roast the weak on a spit, like fishes (16).

This excerpt illustrates the philosophy of statesmanship in the *Mahābhārata.* A monarchy is the only form of government discussed. In return for protection, a king expects taxes which may amount to one-tenth, or one-sixth of the income. He has absolute power and may behave disingenuously if necessary. "For the sake of deceiving the world he should practise very virtuous behavior" (12.58.20). His obligations are to defend the country against foreign oppressors and against robbers, although at times it may be expedient to enlist the robbers' support. Therefore, they should not be dealt with too harshly. On the moral plane, the king receives a fourth part of the merit that his subjects acquire, but also a fourth of all the sin that accumulates in the country (12.67.7,8). This is the nature of the social contract devised by Brahmanical theoreticians. It is more fully expounded in another Sanskrit work, the *Arthaśāstra*.[8]

Indian theories of statesmanship have on occasion been called Macchiavellian in that they preach pragmatic and amoral policies. A king practicing such policies is not motivated by any scruples other than his desire to remain in power. The difference, of course, with Macchiavelli's treatise is that the *Mahābhārata* proclaims its doctrines in the name of Righteousness, whereas the Florentine treatise is avowedly amoral.

II *On Morality in Distress*

In this section of the Book of Peace, problems are discussed pertaining to the ethics of a man who has come upon evil times or is overcome by adversity. Whom do we rely on in times of distress? The answer is given among others, in the form of a parable about a cat who is caught in a hunter's trap and a wise mouse who is being chased by a mongoose and an owl. The mouse suggests he hide himself between the cat's paws where his enemies will not pounce upon him and at the same time he will gnaw the net that keeps the cat captive. This happens and the mouse's enemies soon withdraw disappointed, when the hunter approaches. The mouse, however, waits until the hunter is quite near before he chews the last thread holding the cat. Both escape unharmed, and the cat, who is deeply moved by this act of cooperation, proposes that from then on they be friends: "Be my friend, my counsellor, my father!" But the mouse sadly shakes his head. "When friendships are formed," he answers, "it becomes difficult to determine whether or not the other party is prompted by lust or wrath. There is no such thing as an enemy. There is no such thing in existence as a friend. It is only the force of circumstances that creates friends and enemies. . ." (12.136.134ff.). Elsewhere we read: "As two pieces of wood floating in the ocean come together, then drift apart, so living creatures also meet. Happiness, friends, enemies, are transitory" (12.28.36).

III *On the Morality of Release*

This section of the Book of Peace purports to show, in the main, how to achieve liberation from the bonds of earthly existence. It takes the form of an enumeration of the elements of the universe, their mutual relationships and their moral significance. The human being interacts with these elements in a manner that could either further or detract from his intentions to liberate himself. This book proposes to show both.

In a historical perspective, there are two opinions about the philosophy of the Epic.[9] In one view, that we may call the "transitional," the doctrines of the Epic represent one stage in the evolution of Indian philosophy which develops from the rather disorganized speculations of the *Vedas* and *Upaniṣads* to the mature, coldly logical systems of the later periods. In this view, the *Mokṣadharma* is a unique, half-stage crystallization of philosophical doctrines whose development cannot be ascertained from any work other than the *Mahābhārata*. The often incoherent and self-contradictory philosophical expositions are, therefore, attributable to the groping efforts of imaginative philosophers to construct a world view of their own on the foundations of an antiquated Vedic tradition.

According to a second viewpoint, the Epic's disorganized presentation of philosophical material does not stem from individual efforts of philosophers to unravel the mysteries of release, but from the ignorance of the Epic composers. Many of the philosophical systems were in existence at the time the Epic was growing, according to this theory, but its authors did not quite grasp their complexities and details and so included in their work eclectically as much as they knew of Sāṃkhya. This theory would deny much importance to Epic philosophy.

It is possible to steer a middle course between these extremes by assuming, as for the *Bhagavad-gītā* that the *Mahābhārata* philosophers set out to popularize what they realized was a very intricate philosophy, downgrading it to the level of appreciation of the common man. As such, it becomes a simplified version of the serious thinking that may have taken place at the time. A short excerpt should demonstrate the manner in which the doctrines are expounded: Yudhiṣṭhira has asked Bhīṣma what the *adhyātma-* "super-self" is. After a little digression, Bhīṣma continues:

Earth, wind, space, water and fifthly light are the *mahābhūtas* "gross elements," both the origin and dissolution of all creatures. From those they have been created. Among those creatures the Gross Elements go, time and again, like the waves of the ocean. And just as a turtle, having extended his limbs, withdraws them again, so the World-soul, having sent forth the creatures, withdraws them again. The Creator put the Gross Elements, five only, in all these creatures. The soul beholds that unequal distribution. Sound, hearing and cavities, all three, spring from the womb of Space; from Wind, skin, touch and activity and speech, as a foursome. Form, sight and digestion are called the threefold Energy (Fire). Taste, wetness and the tongue all three are said to be qualities of Water; scent, smell and the body, these three on the other hand are qualities of the earth" (12.187.4-9).

The account continues with a discussion of the mind, the *Buddhi,* and the *Kṣetrajña-* "knower of the field," or soul. They interact with the three *guṇas* "qualities," of the sense organs. This discussion, as well as numerous similar ones, purport to demonstrate which parts of our body, the organs of sense, the mind, etc., interact with what parts of the universe around us. Knowing this we may be a judicious employment of certain of our faculties, avoid such actions as would reinforce the hold that the world exercises on our body and hence on our mind. We should avoid such actions as are suffused with the *guṇas, tamas-* "darkness" and *rajas-* "passion, lust" and only cultivate those illuminated by *sattva-* "goodness."[10] Step by step, the soul will unshackle the bonds of existence, until it ultimately sees the Highest Soul and can unite with it.

This Sāṃkhya theory is supplemented by the Epic Yoga speculations. By strict application of the notion that acts produce *karma,* hence rebirth, we may try to halt the dreary cycle of *saṃsāra-* by abstaining from all activities. The Yogins who sat in hermitages all day and did little else than consume a little food, came closest to the extremist ideal of non-action, i.e., quietism. But the Epic seeks compromises. The most common one is to declare certain acts exempt from *karma* .Those actions which are performed without attachment, i.e., without concern for the results, on the part of the agent, are free from *karma.* Over and over again we read that the truly wise person reacts the same to pain and pleasure, cold and heat, delight and sorrow, remaining unaffected like a waterdrop on the sebaceous leaf of a lotus. This theory can be combined with the Sāṃkhya.

Another compromise which is used to escape the *karma* paradox is that which declares an act of sacrifice exempt from *karma.* Sacrificial acts do not produce *karma,* but instead accrue merit in heaven. A third solution is to perform all one's actions as acts of devotion to the Lord Kṛṣṇa. The latter notion is comparatively late in Indian history and has become very popular as the Bhakti religion spread over India.[11]

It is a difficult and thankless task to determine the exact meaning of every term used in the Epic Sāṃkhya, such as *buddhi, manas, tamas*. The terms are not consistently used. For instance, in one account (12.224-25) the Sāṃkhya explicitly recognizes twenty-five principles: five gross elements, five sense objects, five sense organs, five organs of action, one *manas,* one *ahaṃkāra,* one *buddhi,* one *puruṣa,* and a *prakṛti.* In another account (12.187) as we have seen, such systematization is lacking. In some accounts *buddhi* is qualified by three *guṇas,* in others by eight *bhāvas*. Instances of such variations are numerous. Orientalists and philosophers have frequently discussed whether Sāṃkhya is theistic or non-theistic, whether the *guṇa's* are part of its world view or not, whether it was inspired by Buddhism, or vice versa; in what relationship it stands to the earlier Upaniṣads and to the later, orthodox Sāṃkhya system, and so forth. Few of these problems have been solved definitively. For a more detailed survey of Sāṃkhya philosophy, the reader is referred to the specialist literature.[12]

Other philosophical systems are referred to summarily in the *Mahābhārata*. It places the Sāṃkhya at the same level as Yoga, Veda, Pañcarātra, and Pāśupata (12.337.68), the latter two being sectarian faiths associated with the worship of Viṣṇu and Śiva, respectively. The Pāśupata religion was quite widespread in India at one time. The *Mahābhārata* knows it only as a branch of knowledge taught by Śiva (12.337.62); in the remainder of the Epic the word is used to describe Arjuna's magic weapon.

The name *Pañcarātra* means "five-nights" and refers to the duration of the Vedic human sacrifice, celebrated in the Rig-Vedic Puruṣa hymn. Its doctrines are presented in a rambling, rather confused passage of the Book of Peace (12.322-23). Its adherents worship Nārāyaṇa who is said to be approachable only if one succeeds in reaching the White Island in the Milk Ocean. It can be reached by an unstinting devotion to Nārāyana; hence his followers are called *Ekāntins* "Having one goal (only)." Their acts of devotion consist of folding the hands, loud exclamations of joy and the muttering of prayers. The Universe is said to have evolved from Nārāyaṇa as four emanations (see also 12.336). The twofold god Nara-Nārāyaṇa has been incarnated as Kṛṣṇa and Arjuna (12.326.99 and *passim*). Buddhism is not described, but perhaps indirectly referred to (12.211.32) in the *Mahābhārata.*

The ideal Yogin is a serene, relaxed seeker after release whose sight is directed inward. Occasionally we have a description by a Yogin of his mystical experience, as he stands face to face with the Highest: "Then, like a glowing, smokeless flame, like the brilliant sun; like the fire of lightning in the sky, one beholds the self with the self—and everything seems to be everywhere, because it is pervaded by it . . ." (12.232.18-19).

Many more topics and incidents are related in this curious book. There is obviously no attempt at systematization, but all through miscellaneous and eclectic arguments are used to bring about an atmosphere of solemn morality. If any virtue can be said to be declared paramount, it is that of *ahiṃsā-* "abstention from violence."

CHAPTER 6

The Spread of the Mahābhārata

I *The* Mahābhārata's *Influence in India*

THE *Mahābhārata* has been more influential in the Indian cultural setting than any other literary work, with the possible exception of the *Rāmāyaṇa*. It has been translated into the major Indian languages from early times to the present. In addition, themes, motives, stories, and excerpts from the Great Epic have been used by Sanskrit and vernacular authors, very much in the same way that Greek writers drew upon their ancient store of legends to illustrate contemporary human situations. Religious groups also borrowed from our Epic, often transforming the simple tales until they agreed with their devotional tastes. In the following pages we shall investigate some of these adaptations of the *Mahābhārata* by later authors. It is not possible in the relatively limited space available to give a complete account of the literature and other facets of culture affected by the *Mahābhārata*. We shall confine ourselves to excerpts from literary works based on the *Mahābhārata* which in one way or another have been modified by their authors to conform to their own purpose.

In traditional Hindu estimation, the *Mahābhārata* is part of the non-revealed lore, the *smṛti-*, which means that it is not sacred, as the Vedas are. It is classed together with the Lawbooks, the books on Polity and the *Purāṇas*. It calls itself a history, a *Purāṇa* "ancient tale," a courtly poem, a narration, but not a philosophical treatise.

II *Buddhist Literature*

Although Buddhism spread phenomenally during the reign of King Aśoka (about 250 B.C.) and was still a widespread religion when I-tsing visited India (seventh century A.D.), the *Mahābhārata* contains no reference to the life of the Buddha. On the other hand, in the Buddhist *Jātakas* we find mention of King Dhananjaya Koravya (Kauravya) of Indapatta (Indraprastha) in the Kuru kingdom, with an adviser Vidhūra.[1] In a *gāthā* he is said to have descended from Yuddhiṭṭhila (Yudhiṣṭhira). King Koravya pronounces a diatribe against Brahmans. Elsewhere, Kanhā (=Kṛṣṇā, another name for Draupadī) who is married to the five Pāṇḍu brothers from Takkasilā, is held up as an example of immorality: "Insatiate still she lusted for more/And with a hump-backed dwarf played the whore." [2] For a long time she had a dwarf as a lover and when finally found out, she was abandoned by Yudhitthira and his brothers who were then convinced of the immorality of women. Elsewhere, the mutual extermination of Vṛṣṇis and Andhakas serves as an illustration of the evil effects of alcohol.[3] Stray references occur to other *Mahābhārata* figures, e.g., Kṛṣṇa Dvaipāyana.

In another Buddhist work, the *Buddhacarita* of Aśvaghoṣa,[4] who lived somewhere between 50 B.C. and A.D. 100, the destruction of Kurus and Vṛṣṇi-Andhakas is held up as an instructive example as to how people dominated by their passions meet their doom—the Kurus through their addiction to gambling, the Vṛṣṇi-Andhakas by their alcoholic orgies. King Pāṇḍu similarly fell prey to his lust when he embraced Mādrī. We find indications that other versions of the *Mahābhārata* were current; e.g., Aśvaghoṣa refers to Śantanu's love for Gaṅgā and his grief when she left him, an episode unknown to our Epic. In the philosophical parts of the *Buddhacarita,* Aśvaghoṣa has drawn on the *Śānti-parvan,* usually to contrast his hero's opinion with those of older, false teachers.

These references to the *Mahābhārata* are exceedingly valuable, since they show that the text and many of the incidental stories of the *Mahābhārata* already existed at this rather early date.

III *Sanskrit Literature*

To list the Sanskrit works that refer to, or have been influenced by the *Mahābhārata,* is next to impossible. We shall confine ourselves to a judicious selection.[5]

Perhaps contemporary with Aśvaghoṣa was the dramatist Bhāsa who has left us six plays with themes derived from the *Mahābhārata.*[6] The playwright has altered some of the themes and others he either invented, or drew from a version now lost to us. The drama *Pañcarātra* is based on the battle in the *Virāṭa-parvan;* the *Dūtavākyam* "Ambassador's Report" on Kṛṣṇa's vain mission to the Kuru court to save the peace (*Udyoga-parvan,* 122-30). The *Madhyamavyāyoga* deals with an unknown incident whereby Bhīma meets his monstrous son Ghaṭotkaca who does not recognize him, but takes him to his mother, Bhīma's former mistress. In the *Dūtaghaṭotkaca,* similarly unknown in the Epic, the same Ghaṭotkaca acts as an emissary to try to stop the war when it is half over. The *Karṇābhara* treats of Karṇa's tragic life, how he is deprived of his armor by Indra's treachery. The story is culled from various *parvans* of the *Mahābhārata.* Most famous of Bhāsa's short dramas is the one-act *Ūrubhaṅga* "Thigh-fracture" which tells of Bhīma's fight with Duryodhana on the final day of the battle, whereby the latter has his thighs broken (9.57). As the wounded warrior lies on the battlefield and repents of his evil deeds, he is visited by his mother and father and dissuades Aśvatthāman from undertaking the carnage the next night. This episode is again Bhāsa's invention.

In the following scene from the *Pañcarātra* (2.60-66) Virāṭa has just returned from his successful campaign against the Trigartas and meets his son Uttara who has just come back from his victory over the Kurus with the aid of Arjuna, dressed as a transvestite (*Mbhr.* 4.63).

Uttara: Father, I greet you . . . Let honor be paid to the man who deserves it most.

King: Who, my son?

Uttara: To Dhanaṃjaya (Arjuna) who is standing right here.

King: (*seeing only the transvestite Bṛhannalā*) Why do you say "Dhanaṃjaya"?

Uttara: Because this worthy man, fetched from the graveyard his bow and quivers with imperishable arrows;
The Kings and Bhīsma and the rest were defeated and we were protected (61).

Bṛhannalā: Let the prince be calm, be calm: By his youth, indeed, carried away, he does not even know he was the one who was shooting;
Though having done the whole work himself, he believes it to be another's (62).

Uttara: Please resolve your doubt! This will tell: A scar inflicted by the string of his Gāṇḍiva bow, hidden on his fore-arm,
Which even at the end of twelve years has not blended with the color (of the arm).

(At first, Bṛhannalā maintains his bracelets have caused the scar, but then he proudly states:) "If I am the Bhārata Arjuna, whose body was licked by Rudra's arrows, (then) by implication, that is Bhīmasena, this King Yudhiṣṭhira!"

King: O Dharmarāja! Vṛkodara! Dhanaṃjaya! Why did you not confide in me? . . ."

And so the play continues in Bhāsa's artless, rather plodding style. In the *Mahābhārata* this denouement is actually more vividly related.

The best-known Sanskrit author and dramatist, Kālidāsa, derived the theme of his most famous play, *Śakuntalā,*[7] from the first book of the *Mahābhārata* (1.62-70). He also has made some changes in the story, especially in the characterization of the persons. The King's brutish character is polished a little, since his heartless disavowal of Śakuntalā is ascribed to a curse from an angry sage. Also, the king gives Śakuntalā a ring as he leaves the hermitage, as a token of his faith. She loses the ring which is swallowed by a fish, but reappears when the fish is presented to the king at a critical moment. The king's memory is restored and he searches for Śakuntalā and the boy until he has found them and then installs Bharata on the throne. Kālidāsa's style is refined and genteel compared to the Epic's plain narrative. For instance, the story of Śakuntalā's descent is put in the mouth of one of her companions, but even she is too modest to relate it all.

Another episode of the *Mahābhārata* has been immortalized by the poet Bhāravi's *Kirātārjunīya-,*[8] a seventh-century work that deals with Arjuna's penance on the Himālaya to acquire the divine weapons from the god Śiva (*Mbhr.* 3.39-41). It is an ornate poem in the grand style of the high poetic tradition of Sanskrit. The outline of the epic story has been altered little, but it has been encumbered with elegant disquisitions on statecraft and philosophy, and the text is a tiresome accumulation of similes, alliterations, metaphors, and similar embellishments. The narrative includes elaborate, stereotyped descriptions of forests, mountains, and streams in which minutely described nymphs are dallying.

An example of Bhāravi's massive style is the following extract from the *Kiratārjuniya,* Book Fifteen.

When the Lord (Śiva) shot his arrows at Jiṣṇu (Arjuna), the mountain, replete with the humming of Pināka (Śiva's bow), reverberated, splitting, as it were and resonating in the space around it (34).

With wonder his armies, mountains of varying appearance, as it were, not moving as if painted, looked at the terrible battle between the two (35).

From the mouth and nose of Arjuna, whose efforts were frustrated by Śiva and whose arrows were broken, fire issued forth (46).

The battle proceeds for another canto; Arjuna's bow fails against Śiva, so does his sword. Even when he resorts to throwing rocks and tree trunks, his efforts are fruitless, so that he finally engages Śiva in a fist fight, "pounding with his arms the breast, hard as rock, of the three-eyed one" (17.63). After a while, Śiva reveals himself and "Then Pāṇḍu's son beheld Hara (Śiva) who had assumed his own terrifying shape, adorned with snow-white ashes and illuminated by the disk of the moon on his head, and bowed before him" (18.15). "Slowly the clouds rained down on the earth; colorful heavenly flowers fell from heaven. the sound of a drum struck by nobody filled the clear, shining sky, vigorously" (18.17).

From about the seventh century dates the biographical prose work *Harṣacarita* [9] by Bāṇa, which treats of the life of King Harṣa, a Buddhist ruler who conquered almost the whole of North India (A.D. 606-47). It is unclear whether Bāṇa similarly was a Buddhist. He treats the *Mahābhārata* together with the *Rāmāyana* and the *Purāṇas* as an *āgama-*, a non-religious treatise, but not as a work of philosophy. In his introduction to the *Harṣacarita,* he pays tribute to Vyāsa who sanctified the *Mahābhārata.* Throughout his works, episodes of the *Mahābhārata* are used to illustrate the heroic nature of his characters. For instance, Harṣa's aged general is declared to "surpass even the *Mahābhārata* by the beauty of his manifold exploits of heroism." Harṣa's episodic life is compared to the *Mahābhārata* story, and "hundreds of *Mahābhāratas* would not have sufficed to describe the treasures he (Bāna) saw when merely standing at the gate of Harṣa's palace." There is one reference to *Śvetadvīpa* the "White Island" where Nārāyaṇa was worshipped, but nowhere is Kṛṣṇa identified with Viṣṇu.[10] However, at approximately the same time the philosopher Śaṃkara composed his monumental commentary on the *Bhagavad-gītā* [11] which set the tone for the further "spiritualization" of the *Mahābhārata.*

Another Sanskrit author, Māgha, who composed a famous heroic poem, *Śiśupālavadha* [12] "Murder of Śiśupāla," in the latter part of the seventh century, was a devout worshipper of Kṛṣṇa. He conceived of his work as a means of glorifying his Lord. From his point of view, the slaying of the rebellious Śiśupāla (*Mhbr.* 2.37-42) who objects to the award Kṛṣṇa receives at Yudhiṣṭhira's royal consecration, is an act of divine clemency on the part of Kṛṣṇa, benefiting Śiśupāla's own soul. By the strange dialectic of the Kṛṣṇa devotee the soul of a person hating the Lord unites with him after death. Besides spinning out the details of the consecration to a great length, Māgha introduces a few variations into the *Mahābhārata* story which are of no great importance. One of the most interesting episodes is Śiśupāla's imprecation of Kṛṣṇa after he has been offered and has accepted the guest honor. Through a skillful manipulation of the Sanskrit language Māgha imparts a double meaning to every one of Śiśupāla's bitter insults, so that it can also be interpreted as an eloquent praise:

Then and there, the ruler of Cedi deemed the honor extended by Pāṇḍu's son (Yudhiṣṭhira) to Madhu's enemy (Kṛṣṇa) in the assembly hall intolerable, for a proud man's heart experiences envy when another is elevated (15.1).

Menacing the whole troop of warriors at the same time, he slowly wagged his head flashing the jewels in his diadem and shaking the three worlds violently (15.3).

His two round shoulders resembled two closely joined mountain peaks. Seizing a pillar he shook it so that it and the whole assembly hall trembled (6).

Flushing deeply, committed to violence and unheedful of danger, his eye clung to the sword on his side, just as an enamored girl relies on the female companion at her side (9).

This fearless man whose deep voice resembled the thunder of a raincloud, declaimed the following speech which reverberated in the hall and whose syllables sounded very clearly and distinctly (13):

"If a person is honored, it is in deference to some outstanding virtue. What is the purpose, O King of Kurus, of honoring Hari (Kṛṣṇa) who is in want of virtues (or: free from the three guṇas)?" (15.1).

People call him a yokel, devoid of all skills, unacquainted with emotions and sentiments, living outside the city and uneducated (or: The people call him "knower of the field," free from all ignorance, unacquainted with desires and sensual proclivities, to be supported by the city, who is not cunning) (3).

Hard-hearted, irresponsible, he always finds satisfaction in repressing affection for his friends and clansmen, although they are devoted to him (or: Tranquil at heart, indifferent to wealth, poverty, etc. and repressing the desires in his friends, kin and clansmen, he attains happiness) (12).

The attending kings become restless and excited. Śiśupāla urges them to slay "that servant of Kaṃsa together with those five scoundrels and this old maid of a king (Bhīṣma)" (15.63). Śiśupāla and Kṛṣṇa declare war and go home to muster their respective armies. A battle ensues with scenes as bloody, but more lyrical than those of the *Mahābhārata*. In the end Kṛṣṇa kills Śiśupāla with his disk and "Then the kings saw with wonder how from Caidya's (Śiśupāla's) body a spirit detached itself excelling the sun in brilliance. It entered into Kṛṣṇa's body, worshipped by Śrī" (20.79). Here the poem ends.

The philosopher Kumārila of the seventh or eighth century A.D. saw in the Epic not so much the struggle between hostile factions, but rather an exposition by Vyāsa of the duties of the warrior caste in war and peace. The battle story is, therefore, only incidental to the didactic theme of the *Mahābhārata*. He believed the episodes were introduced with the definite aim of illustrating a moral principle for the listener. That they provided enjoyment as well was unimportant.[13]

The late eighth century saw the dramatization of the epic story at the hand of the poet Bhaṭṭa Nārāyaṇa, in his work, the *Veṇīsaṃhāra* [14] "Tying of the Hair." The title refers to an invented incident whereby Bhīma, after killing Duryodhana, binds up the hair of Draupadī who had vowed to leave it hanging in a braid until the injury done her at the gambling match, had been righted. The central theme, as is evident, revolves around a heroic incident. The drama is in six acts and covers the action from the fifth to the twelfth books of the *Mahābhārata*. The poet is straightforward in his descriptions and unhampered by considerations of *ahiṃsā* and other ethical doctrines. As such it is perhaps the last expression of a truly heroic tradition of which the *Mahābhārata* is the principle example in Sanskrit literature.

Bhīma here is the hero, an unlovable, tough, vengeful warrior determined to go to extremes in order to pay back the insult done to his wife and clan. The description of the battle has the Epic imagery with rivers of blood flowing hither and yon. The one concession Nārāyaṇa has made to pure Hindu tradition is that Bhīma, an Aryan, does not drink Duḥśāsana's blood, but a demon enters the body and drinks it for him. The drama is in weighty language, full of lengthy compounds which make it practically unstageable.[15]

More contrived and refined is the long poem of 2800 stanzas, the *Naiṣadhacarita* [16] by Śrīharṣa, a twelfth-century work of the class *Mahākāvya* "great ornate poetry" to which the *Śiśupālavadha* also belongs. It is based on a portion of the Nala episode of the *Mahā-*

bhārata, which it covers from its inception to the wedding of Nala and Damayantī and the arrival of the evil Kali in the city. The poet has introduced many alterations in arrangement and has also omitted and added parts. Small incidents, like Damayantī's *svayaṃvara* have been spun out to great length, giving the author an excuse to display his skill at constructing figures of speech prescribed by the textbooks. The poem is largely erotic in tone and demonstrates one of the many uses to which the *Mahābhārata* has been put in the course of its literary history. In addition there are oblique references to the Indian philosophical systems.

The following is a brief excerpt from the events after Nala's wedding when he has taken Damayantī back to his capital and she comes to live with him:

> Bending herself, she blew out the burning light with the breath of her mouth, when her beloved pulled her scarf. But, with wonder she saw the regions around her lit up by her consort's crown-jewel (18.85).

> Looking and looking again at her, he looked at her more and more in joy. Embracing her more than once he embraced her again. Though he had kissed her eagerly did he kiss her again. But in no wise was satiety to be found (18.106).

The poem, true to its erotic sentiment, elaborates the love scenes more than the translator considered delicate. All this is foreign to the austere *Mahābhārata.*

Among other evaluations of our text is the one by Ānandavardhana, the author of a ninth-century work on the theory of poetry, *Dhvanyāloka.*[17] He holds that the *Mahābhārata* has many tones and moods, but that to characterize its main tone (*rasa*), we have to class it in the category *Śānti* "peace." The work affords the listener or reader peace of mind and tranquillity. Similar sentiments are expressed by the theoreticians Abhinavagupta and Kṣsmendra. From their point of view, peace is the ultimate outcome of the strife, war, victory, and suffering of the Pāṇḍavas and their adversaries.

In the branch of Sanskrit narrative literature, the so-called *ākhyāna* tradition, we again find many of the *Mahābhārata* stories and even entire verses. It is not always certain whether or not those stories derive from an independent tradition. The *Hitopadeśa,*[18] a prose work of fables interspersed with stanzas, has borrowed forty-one of its seven hundred and six stanzas from books twelve and thirteen of the *Mahābhārata;* another thirty-nine from the other books.[19]

Other prose fables have clearly been inspired by our Epic. In the eleventh-century cycle of stories entitled *Kathāsaritsāgara*[20] "Ocean of Stories," each story is a fable containing a pearl of popular wisdom. Here we find the "Vice of Hunting" exemplified by the story of King Pāṇḍu killing the deer (*Mhbr.* 1.109). The story of Nala and Damayantī serves to show that fortunes may vary, just as the sun goes down and then rises again (*Kths.* 9.6.236.416). The snakes licking the sharp *kuśa* grass and getting their tongues split is an example of well-deserved punishment for greed (*Mbhr.* 1.30). These and similar tales have been culled from books one, five, and twelve of the *Mahābhārata.*

The relation of the Sanskrit Lawbooks to the *Mahābhārata* has been an often disputed issue.[21] Manu's Lawbook[22] contains 2685 verses of which about one hundred are quoted almost literally in the twelfth and thirteenth books of the Epic and another twenty-five or so express the same injunctions. Manu is referred to repeatedly in the *Mahābhārata,* but it never mentions our Epic. In all likelihood, the Epic composer of the didactic books was familiar with a code of Manu which differed but little from the extant one. Perhaps there also was at one time a book on statecraft by Manu, from which our Epic has drawn. The other great work on statecraft, the *Arthaśāstra,*[23] shows very little influence from the *Mahābhārata.* The many different lawbooks, on the other hand, often agree in phraseology and content.

Besides these esthetic and moral adaptations of stories or incidents from the *Mahābhārata,* its themes have been freely used in religious works also, often with astonishing distortions of the textual material. More than any other genre, the *Purāṇas* have borrowed from the *Mahābhārata.* Of the eighteen traditional *Purāṇas,* six celebrate the greatness of Viṣṇu, or Kṛṣṇa. In the most famous of these, the *Bhāgavata-purāṇa*[24] (between A.D. 300 and 500?) the Lord Kṛṣṇa is represented as a *bhakti*-hero, an object of devotion. He is worshipped in many forms in this *Purāṇa,* as a cute infant, beloved to his mother, as a prankish boy, as a mystic lover with a flute, as a slayer of demons and as the benevolent, gracious teacher of religion. Only in the last capacity is he known to the *Mahābhārata,* the remainder are Purāṇic stories. Episodes from the *Mahābhārata* are selected as examples of devotional behavior. In the *Bhagavata-purāṇa,* for instance, Jarāsaṃdha, as in the *Mahābhārata,* is killed by Bhīma (*Mbhr.* 2.18-22), but Kṛṣṇa is credited with the release of the imprisoned kings from their dungeon. As they emerge, they see Kṛṣṇa and "drink Him as it were with their eyes, lick Him as it were with their tongues, smell Him as it were with their nostrils, embrace Him as it were with their arms. They bend down with their heads, their sins destroyed, to the feet of Hari . . . With their voices and clasped hands, they laud Hṛṣikeśa" (10.73.5f.). Then follows a lengthy hymn of praise.

Another favorite devotional episode is Draupadī's prayer to Kṛṣṇa at the time she is undressed during the gambling match. The *Mahābhārata* does not know this prayer. Also, Sāvitrī's devotion to her husband Satyavant is held up as an instance of exemplary wifely devotion. Arjuna's relation to Kṛṣṇa at the time the latter utters the *Bhagavad-gītā,* is often interpreted as that of a devotee and his god.

As can be expected, Purāṇic literature devoted to Śiva is less prone to borrow from the *Mahābhārata* than the Vaiṣṇavite *Purāṇas.* In one work, however, the *Kūrma-purāṇa,* a song of devotion to Śiva occurs, the *Iśvara-gītā,*[25] which is clearly inspired by the *Bhagavad-gītā.* Here Viṣṇu is also the Lord, but he is declared to be inferior to Śiva.

It is often difficult to determine whether a later adaptation of a *Mahābhārata* incident has been borrowed from the original work, or from a Purāṇic account. To prove it one way or another is a problem of text criticism that lies outside the scope of this work. In all further discussions we have to bear in mind that the *Purāṇas* could have been the source for isolated incidents and stories.

The philosopher Madhva (1197-1276) considered the *Mahābhārata* one of the greatest works of literature. To him it is a spiritual work of such profundity that gods even cannot fathom it. Like Sukthankar (see Chapter 3) he recognizes three levels on which the Epic is significant. The *āstika,* or historical meaning, first of all, is expressed by the adventures of the Pāṇḍavas and Kṛṣṇa as we read them. In the second place, the religious meaning is found in the discourses on philosophy and religion, ethics, and proper behavior. He refers to this level as *manvādi,* meaning that it was taught by Manu. Thirdly, the *auparicara* meaning, lit., "oriented towards transcendency" is expressed by the invocations of God and his names. In its totality, its meaning is spiritual and closely associated with the branches of wisdom in the *Vedas.*

Madhva's favorite hero was Bhīma, the son of the Windgod Vāyu: He sees the heroes of the battle as symbolizations of mental properties: Vāyu's incarnation, Bhīma, stands for *prāṇa* "life-breath," with its properties of piety, wisdom, renunciation, resolution, and so on. Draupadī, as an incarnation of Sarasvatī, represents wisdom on earth. The other Pāṇḍavas stand for meritorious acts. On the opposite side, Duryodhana, the incarnation of Kali, represents unwisdom, Duḥśāsana perverted wisdom, Śakuni heresy, and the other warriors sins. Viṣṇu-Kṛṣṇa is the good party's charioteer, i.e., leader.[26]

IV *Jain Literature*

The sect called Jains is about as ancient as Buddhism and has a religion based on rigid percepts of personal conduct and the veneration of Jain saints. Their literature is vast in extent and not always sympathetic to Hinduism, as may be judged from the quotation on p. 46. But Jains do incorporate ancient Hindu heroes into their religious writings. Often the stories are altered in such a manner that the heroes act and think as devout Jains. Adaptations from the *Mahābhārata* are not abundant.

In one of the oldest Jain canonical texts, the *Jñātadharmakathā,*[27] Draupadī, here called Dovaī, is said to be a former incarnation of the nineteenth Tīrthaṅkara, Malli. Before her *svayaṃvara,* she pays homage to the Jain images and then chooses the Pāṇḍavas by modestly catching their reflections in a mirror, rather than facing them. She declares all five to be her husbands. Later, in Hastināpura, the evil sage Nārada visits her and as the result of an imagined slight from Dovaī, he arranges to have her kidnapped by a king from Amarakaṅka. Kṛṣṇa rescues her. Later he becomes angry with the Pāṇḍu brothers and curses them that they cannot return to their capital. Instead, they go south, enter a Jain order and after many years fast themselves to death.

In a non-canonical work, the *Dharmaparīkṣā*[28] (A.D. 1014), we read that Gāndhāri became pregnant after embracing a breadfruit tree and so gave birth to one hundred sons. Arjuna enters the underworld by shooting a hole in the ground with his arrows and fetches the king of snakes from his subterranean abode to present him to Yudhiṣṭhira. Karṇa is born to Kuntī and Pāṇḍu as the result of a premarital affair, and her mother puts him in a basket and lets it float down the Ganges. The king of Campā adopts him.

The great battle is fought between the army of Kṛṣṇa and Duryodhana. Kṛṣṇa becomes ruler of the world and all ultimately go to the Jains' heaven.

The famous scholar Hemacandra composed a monumental "History of the Sixty-three Holy Men"[29] (A.D. 1160-72) in which he draws on a few *Mahābhārata* stories. Kṛṣṇa is portrayed as a cousin of Ariṣṭanemi, the twenty-second Pārśva. They are friends and wander over the world preaching the Jain creed. The episode of Jarāsaṃdha's quarrel (*Mbhr.* 2.22) is reworked so that he is defeated only after a full-scale battle with Kṛṣṇa as in the Harivaṃśa (Ch. 171). Jarāsaṃdha is supported by Dhṛtarāṣṭra's sons and Kṛṣṇa and Ariṣṭanemi by the Pāṇḍavas. When Ariṣṭanemi sounds his formidable conchshell to rally Kṛṣṇa's army, he kills one hundred thousand enemies by the mere power of the noise. Śiśupāla is among those slain on the battlefield, unlike in the Epic. A discus hurled by Kṛṣṇa kills Jarāsaṃdha, but his spirit does not fuse with that of Kṛṣṇa and goes to the fourth hell, instead. The kings in fief to Jarāsaṃdha are liberated and pay worship to Ariṣṭanemi. Elsewhere in this work, Draupadī is abducted from Hastināpura by a king from Campā for having been impolite to the sage Nārada. She is rescued by Kṛṣṇa.

A version of the Nala story also appears in the *Triṣaṣṭiśalākā-puruṣacaritra:* here the heroine is Davadantī; the incident with the gods at the *svayaṃvara* does not take place at all, but instead a door-keeper announces the guests. Davadantī places the wreath around Nala's neck, much to the chagrin of a man named Kṛṣṇarāja who out of jealousy seeks to kill him. Davadantī, however, quenches the flaring battle spirit with a douse of water thrown on the quarrelers. They settle their fight. Nala then conquers the city of Takṣaśilā and loses it again by gambling (p. 274ff.). An epitome of the *Mahābhārata* showing many modifications, the *Pāṇḍavacarita* by Devprabha Sūri, was composed in the thirteenth century. In A.D. 1551 Śubhacandra wrote the Pāṇḍavapurāṇa, also called the "Jains' Mahābhārata." The Kannaḍa translation of the *Mahābhārata* is also by a Jain (see p. 102). In the *Kathākośa,*[30] a late poem in bad Sanskrit interspersed with Prākrit, the story of Nala and Davadantī also appears in a light-hearted form. When Davadantī chooses her husband, she makes light of her suitors. Upon being introduced to the King of Gauḍa, she comments to the butler: "The color of this man is black and horrible, like that of elephants—so pass on quickly."[31]

V *The Aryan Vernaculars*

Sanskrit remained understandable to the cultured and semicultured for a considerable period of time after it had ceased to be a spoken language. Ultimately, however, the vernaculars evolved too far to show much similarity with Sanskrit [32] and the mass of the people who wished to listen to the *Mahābhārata,* would have to rely on translations into their native tongues. Often more than one translation was made and often only partial translations. Some are literal and formal, obviously the product of the erudite upper class, others are free renderings, with additions, omissions, modifications in arrangement, abridgements, and expansions. One of the earliest is the *Mahābhārata* in the Orīyan language composed by an illiterate peasant, Saralā Dāsa [33] (fifteenth century). He is said to have heard it recited once and then to have made embellishments of his own. His interpretation is that of a flesh-and-blood epic where ambitious men strive for conquest and women intrigue for social position. It is a fresh, vigorous reworking of our Epic and has retained its popularity to the present day. The philosophical portions have been blithely ignored. Later translations of the *Mahābhārata* in Orissa have not acquired the same popularity as Saralā Dāsa's common-sense epic. Saralā Dāsa for instance, arranges an emotional scene when Draupadī meets Bhīma's former lover, Hiḍimbā. The two women quarrel and hurl insults at one another, like village women. He incorporates the geography known to him into the Epic. The influence of Saralā's epic on Orīyan life and literature has been great, and it has also been translated into Bengalī.

The best and most popular translation of the *Mahābhārata* into Bengalī, however, is from the hand of Kāśīram Dās, a schoolmaster (about A.D. 1650). As in the Orīyan version, this work does not follow the Sanskrit original very closely and treats of its subject matter in a down-to-earth, simple manner.[34] Kāśīrām Dās was not very concerned about the epic philosophy, although he shows great reverence toward Brahmans. Occasionally, he introduces incidents from his daily experience, as when Yudhiṣṭhira, during his coronation sacrifice, is visited by King Joy Sen of Giribraja (Bhāgalpur). Kṛṣṇa is revered as the supereme being, and since the *Mahābhārata* does not afford much scope for such reverence, Kāśīrām invents incidents. When the King of Laṅkā refuses to bow to Yudhiṣṭhira, asserting that he will only bow his head before Kṛṣṇa, Kṛṣṇa quickly places himself behind Yudhiṣṭhira's throne and shows himself in all his divine glory. Every onlooker, including the refractory king, falls on his face so that Kṛṣṇa can declare Yudhiṣṭhira the mightiest of all emperors.[35]

Numerous other partial or complete translations of the *Mahā-*

bhārata in Bengalī exist. No less than thirty-one authors have undertaken them, from the fourteenth century onward. The most remarkable is the one composed under the patronage of the Mohammedan ruler Husain Shāh (1494-1520). It shows the interest this ruler took in Hindu culture. One of his generals, Parāgul, also appears in it.

The earliest literary works of *Assam* [36] are the popular *Jayadrathbadh* "Slaying of Jayadratha" (*Mbhr.* 7.121) by Kaviratna Sarasvatī and two other narratives derived from our Epic, Harivara Vipra's *Vabrubāhar Yuddha* from *Mbhr.* 14.78 and the *Sātyaki Praveśa* based on an incident from the *Droṇa-parvan.* Verses from these works were sung by the Ojāpālis, the leaders of the village choruses. But with the appearance of the Bhakti author Mahapurush Srimanta Sankardeva (1449-1568), a more serious *Mahābhārata* tradition became more popular celebrating devotion to Lord Kṛṣṇa. Sankardeva himself drew his inspiration from the *Bhāgavata-purāṇa,* but under King Naranārāyana (1540-85) all the books except the *Strī-* and *Anuśāsana-parvans* were translated into Assamese verse, by Rāma Sarasvatī. The king participated actively in this work and is frequently eulogized. It is a religious, Vaiṣṇavite poem in Assam and is apparently never sung by the Ojāpālis. Very popular has become Draupadī's lament to Kṛṣṇa as he is about to depart to the Kurus on a mission of peace. The translation seems to be faithful except for minor differences, such as the Pāṇḍavas' fight with a goat-faced demon Kulācala and Draupadī killing a lion with her bangle under Kṛṣṇa's inspiration.

Also in the sixteenth century the *Mahābhārata* was translated into Hindī and Gujarātī. The seventeenth century saw a translation into Marāṭhī, although the oldest important work in that language is the thirteenth-century commentary on the *Bhagavad-gītā* by Jñāneśvara, who lived to be only twenty-two years old. The most appreciated versions of the *Mahābhārata* in Marāṭhī are those of Mukteśvar (d. 1660), of which six *parvans* remain, and of Moropant (d. 1749), a version in *āryā* meter.

VI *The Dravidian Languages*

In the languages of southern India, the *Mahābhārata* often occupies the unique place of being the oldest major literary work in a language. This situation applies to Telugu,[37] a language that numbers more speakers than any other of the Dravidian languages. The earliest references to *Mahābhārata* characters are found in the *Tevāram,* a devotional work by the itinerant bard Sundaramūrti (about A.D. 800). He cites the penance of Aruccunar "Arjuna" to gain the Pāśupata weapon (*Mbhr.* 3.38-42) as an example of the might of Śiva: even Bhīma could not have helped Arjuna acquire the weapon, but great Śiva could. The *Mahābhārata,* called *Āndhra Bhāratamu,* was translated through the efforts of three poets, Nannayabhaṭṭa who began it in the eleventh century; Tikkana Somayājī of the thirteenth century and Errana of the fourteenth. Nannaya translated the first two *parvans* and part of the third, rather freely and paying more attention to poetic beauty than to literalness. His language is a greatly Sanskritized metrical prose, employing proper Telugu meters. He excelled in descriptions of nature which in his version he liberally expanded. His successors used a less Sanskritized language. All were much caught up in the devotional movement which was spreading through India at the time. The entire translation consists of fifty thousand stanzas.

One of the great later *kāvyas* in Telugu literature, the *Vijayavilāsa* by Chemākūn Venkatakavi (seventeenth century), deals with Arjuna's tour of the holy places and his marriages to Ulūpī and Subhadrā.

In Kannaḍa [38] literature, the *Mahābhārata* was translated as early as A.D. 902 in its Jain version as the *Pampabhārata,* or *Vikramārjunavijaya.* Arjuna here has become the principle hero of the Epic. Every chapter begins with a praise in his honor and ends with a panegyric of his prowess. Draupadī is Arjuna's wife only. He is crowned after the Bhārata war with Subhadrā as his queen. Pampa desired to sing the glory of his patron, Arikesari II, who had distinguished himself in a successful war against a tyrant, just as Arjuna had done.

The *Pampabhārata* is a concatenation of scenes which together give a continuous story rather than a translation of the *Mahābhārata.* Second to Arjuna, Karṇa appears as a hero. He is tender to his mother, loyal to his masters and faces his tragic fate with proper resignation.[39] Kṛṣṇa is not prominent in his work, as it is not influenced by the Bhakti movement. It was left to the fifteenth-century poet Kumāra Vyāsa to transform the Epic into a *Kṛṣṇa-bhakti,* in Kannaḍa meters.[40] His work, which abounds in metaphors, is still popular. The Epic figures are also used in much cruder folk plays, called *Yaksha Gaṇas.*[41]

Tamil, the language with the richest native literary treasure of all Dravidian languages, has not experienced as radical an influence from the *Mahābhārata* as the other languages. An eighth-century Tamil inscription states that the *Mahābhārata* had been translated into Tamil. The earliest known translation by Perum Devanār (eighth century) is only preserved in parts, e.g., the *Udyoga-parvan.* But sundry quotations in Tamil from later commentators are not taken from Perum Devanār's work, but from an unknown source. This may or may not be the one referred to in the inscription. In the fourteenth century an epitome, the *Villiputturār-Bhāratam,* appeared. A modern Tamil reworking of this epitome was published by C. Rājagopalachari as *Viyāsar Virundu* (1943) in 107 episodes. The English translation of this work is quite popular in India, but is for us more difficult to appreciate because of the author's frequent private moralistic digressions. As in the other languages, the *Mahābhārata* stories are quite well-known in Tamil, although they tend to be overshadowed by the strongly devotional lyrics of the Tamil saints.

In Malayālam literature, the *Rāmāyaṇa* was translated much earlier than the *Mahābhārata.* In the sixteenth-century *campūs,* mixed prose-verse hymns, many *Mahābhārata* themes were used, but the work was not translated until the seventeenth century, by Tuñchattu Rāmānuja Ezhuttachan, who condensed it. The *Tuḷḷal* "dance drama" of the eighteenth century adopted many *Mahābhārata* themes, and modern dramas, novels, and stories occasionally do also.[42]

VII *The* Mahābhārata *in Southeast Asia*

Outside India the stories of the Sanskrit Epics are referred to in the many parts of Asia which have undergone the influence of Hindu culture, i.e., Burma, Thailand, Indo-China and Indonesia. In some of these regions, it is not the *Mahābhārata* but the *Rāmāyaṇa* that has gained a stronger foothold in the receiving country; elsewhere, both epics subsist side by side, and in a few areas all vestiges of the epics have vanished.

At an early time, we do not exactly know how early, Indian merchants established trade contacts with countries outside their subcontinent. Trade routes led to Central Asia, the West, to China, Ceylon, and Southeast Asia. The routes to Southeast Asia and Indonesia lay largely overland, beginning in East Bengal and Assam and thence to Burma and the Malay Peninsula. Sea routes existed from the main ports of India. The merchants established trading posts where they were soon joined by priests and bards who helped spread Indian culture. As the trading post became more influential, a Hindu ruler would take over the government and establish a dynasty which gradually Hinduized the native population. Politically, we then would have a Hindu royal house ruling over a native population of different racial stock and culture. The Hindu and native cultures would ultimately blend and assume a character of their own. As a result, there are often two versions of a literary work, the original Sanskrit, with or without translation, and a native adaption in the language of the country. The literature based on or inspired by the Indian original is not in Sanskrit.

Most of the cultural influence of India in the countries surrounding it, has not been in the form of Hinduism, but of Buddhism. The emperor Aśoka introduced Buddhism to Ceylon, and Burma received it before the sixth century A.D. from missionaries. In Thailand, Burma, and Indo-China direct references to the *Mahābhārata* are rare. Indirect references, such as the names of *Mahābhārata* figures and gods and allusions to incidents are almost entirely lacking. A sixth-century Thai inscription reads that a Brahman, Somaśarma by name, had the *Rāmāyaṇa, Purāṇas,* and the *Mahābhārata* performed and arranged for daily recitations without interruption. But on the whole, Burma and Thailand have found the *Rāmāyaṇa* and its incidents of greater appeal than the *Mahābhārata.* If in these countries the *Mahābhārata* has been known and has been the source of inspiration for works of literature and art, no traces of such influence have been reported.

In Cambodia and Indonesia the situation is different. Here, for reasons unknown, the Great Epic has been accepted as part of the national cultural stock, together with the *Rāmāyaṇa.* We shall confine ourselves to a discussion of these countries.

Cambodia. This country has been independent for a long time. The Chinese called it Fu-nan as early as the first century A.D. when it included modern Laos also. The kings have Sanskrit names from the sixth century on. According to an old tradition, the kingdom of Campā (Vietnam) was founded in the following manner: "The illustrious Śrī Jayaddharma, mighty and courageous, went to Bhavapura (Cambodia). There Kauṇḍinya, that foremost of Brahmans, had planted a spear which he had obtained from Aśvatthāman, son of Droṇa." [43] Two Śaivite sects, the Pāśupatas and the Śaivites, practiced their religion in the country. Both are known from the *Mahābhārata*. The Pāśupatas seem to have flourished as wandering monks, and the Śaivites may have been instrumental in establishing numerous temples to Śiva Mahāliṅga. From inscriptions we learn that the Indian epics and *Purāṇas* enjoyed popularity. Quotations are not recorded, but statuary confirms it. In the ninth century the name Bhṛgu, a well-known sage from the *Mahābhārata,* is given to the mythical forefather of the Campā dynasty in Laos.[44]

In later times, Śaivism and Vaiṣṇavism in Cambodia, just as in Indonesia, fused into what is called Brahmanism, as opposed to Buddhism. A corresponding amalgamation of the deities Viṣṇu and Śiva cannot be traced to the *Mahābhārata* where they are kept strictly separate. Only in the *Harivaṃśa* (181) Śiva, and Viṣṇu are said to be the same, Harihara.

More tangible than these indirect references are the testimonies we find in Cambodian art. Part of the famous Angkor complex was constructed over a period of about four hundred years, from c.800 to c.1200. The temple of Angkor Wat was built by King Suryavarman II after he had returned from a conquest of Campā and the Malay Peninsula. The bas-reliefs in the walls of the galleries of the first story illustrate several stories in the *Mahābhārata*. We find here the churning of the ocean (*Mhbr*. 1.15-17) and its accompanying anecdotes, the emergence of the moon, Lakṣmī, the horse Uccaiḥśravas, the jewel Kaustubha and finally, the *amṛta*. In the *Mahābhārata* account, the Devas pull at the head of the snake Vāsuki, whereas the Asuras hold the tail. In this relief the situation is reversed. Also, Viṣṇu is here shown to carry off the world poison, an incident not found in the *Mahābhārata*.

In the southern part of the western gallery is a magnificent scene depicting the clash of the Pāṇḍava and Kuru forces on the battlefield. The whole of Angkor Wat portrays incidents from Viṣṇu's *avatāras* and so it should not surprise us to find Kṛṣṇa as a four-armed charioteer steering Arjuna's carriage. Bhīṣma pierced with arrows, lies on the field of battle, apparently delivering his speeches of wisdom. The long lines of chariot horses rearing up, the proud warriors hurling their deadly missiles, the battle elephants furiously rushing at one another, all are sculpted in a truly heroic style worthy of the Epic.

Elsewhere, at the entrance to the south gate of Angkor Thom, is another representation of the churning of the ocean. It was erected by a Buddhist king, Jayavarman VII (1181-1220), who by his persistent battles with the Chams and his lavish expenditures on architecture, exhausted the kingdom's funds. In conception it is grandiose: the gate is the mountain Mandara which, being churned by the Devas and Asuras flanking the causeway, produces wealth for the king of Cambodia. In execution it is equally overwhelming and powerful. Undoubtedly, it is here in Cambodia that we find the most magnificent works of art inspired by the *Mahābhārata* that can be found anywhere, either in India or outside of it.

Undoubtedly, Sanskrit literature has left other traces in Cambodian literature. The literature of Laos, for one thing, has been strongly influenced by Indian literature in general from the sixteenth century on, not only in content, such as the introduction of Hindu gods and Buddhist divinities into their native tales, but also in the poetic form. Classical Laotian poetry has adopted the Indian metrical system of distichs with caesura, whereas their earliest epics were constructed in verses with assonance and rhythm. Indra functions often as a kind of fate or Providence.[45] But as it is our intention to trace specifically the features referable to the *Mahābhārata,* it is superfluous to give details. The *Rāmāyaṇa* has been equally, if not more, influential.

Indonesia. In tracing the history of the Epic in Indonesia, we tread on firmer ground than in Cambodia or Laos, for the *Mahābhārata* has enjoyed a great popularity among the people of Java and Bali. We shall confine ourselves to these two islands, for it is here and on Sumatra that most of the cultural development of this great archipelago has taken place.[46]

The commercial relations between India and Indonesia go back to unknown times. Ptolemy (first century A.D.) knew of a *Iabadiū,* or *Sabadiū,* the Greek versions of the Sanskrit *Yavadvīpa* (Java), but its earliest recorded reference in Indian literature is in the *Rāmāyaṇa*[47] (4.39.28) of perhaps the third century A.D. where it is called, as is common for distant places "rich in jewels, adorned by seven kingdoms." The earliest reference to Bali is found in the Buddhist cyclopaedia *Tantra-Mañjuśrīmūlakalpa,* probably a seventh-century work, where it is mentioned along with *Vārūṣaka* "Sumatra" and *Yavadvīpa*. It is called Bāli.

The earliest Sanskrit inscription on Java dates from the fifth century, from a King Pūrṇavarman, Lord of the town of Tārumā. The next dated inscription is from Central Java (A.D. 733) and celebrates the establishment of a *liṅga*. Some time in this period, Buddhism in its Mahāyānic and Tantric forms was introduced to Java.

Brahmanism and Buddhism existed side-by-side. To Buddhism we owe the magnificent Borobudur. We also owe to it a copperplate inscription from Nālandā, a Buddhist university near Benares, India, which attests to the active intercourse between India and Indonesia in the ninth century. The inscription commemorates the establishment of a Buddhist monastery by a king Bālaputradeva of Java (*Yavabhūmi*) whose son "was the foremost warrior on battlefields and his fame was equal to that acquired by Yudhiṣṭhira, Parāśara, Bhīmasena, Karṇṇa and Arjjuna." [48] Apparently the king, or rather his long-winded court-poet, held no scruples about borrowing heroic examples from the Hindu epic to illustrate the very un-Buddhistic virtues of his patron.

By the time of the reign of Anantavikrama of East Java (latter part of the tenth century), Java was a prosperous, thoroughly Hinduized country, with temples and shrines to Hindu deities and Indian geographical names.[49] The Hindu Epics had been introduced and were apparently well-received by the Javanese, for the king undertook to have the *Mahābhārata* translated into the language of the country, the language we now call Old Javanese.

The Old Javanese Mahābhārata. Not all the books of the Old Javanese *Mahābhārata* have survived.[50] That there were, as in the Indian original, eighteen books, is certain because the Index in the *Ādi-parva* lists them.[51] But in every list the *Anuśāsana-parva* is missing and instead, the *Śalya-parva* is divided into two books, the *Śalya* and the *Gadā*. The latter describes Duryodhana's mace fight with Bhīma. Of the extant books, the following have been published: [52] *Ādi-parva, Virāṭa-parva, Udyoga-parva, Bhīṣma-parva, Āśramavasana-parva, Musala-parva, Prasthānika-parva,* and *Svargārohaṇa-parva.* Of these eight, at least three had been translated by A.D. 1000. Another four exist in manuscript form but have not been published yet.

The actual translation of the work is in Old Javanese prose, a highly Sanskritized court language. Like many of its sister adaptations in India, it is not a literal translation of the Sanskrit, but more a diluted abstract with many incidents omitted or condensed. It has no great literary merit, especially since it has come down in a greatly corrupted form, the scribes being frequently ignorant of Sanskrit. Efforts to reconstruct the text are at most, tentative. But its lack of intrinsic significance is fully compensated for by its unparalleled influence on the subsequent development of Javanese culture. The *Ādi-parva* and the *Virāṭa-parva* have been a source of many *wayang-*

purva themes, the *Udyoga-* and *Bhīṣma-parvas* furnished materials for an Old Javanese epic, the *Bhārata-Yuddha,* and others. Books on law and conduct, like the *Agastya-parva* also borrowed from the *Mahābhārata.*

The *Ādi-parva* contains most of the episodes of the Sanskrit original. Among them are the *Pauṣya-parva* (*Mbhr.* 1.3), the episode of Pulomā and Cyavana, Pramadvarā (here called Pramathanā) and Ruru (1.11-13); Jaratkāru who married his namesake (1.41-44), i.e., the second version of the Sanskrit; the churning of the ocean, preceded by the birth of Garuḍa from Kadrū and Vinatā (1.13-40), all of which is related in great detail; the snake sacrifice (1.45-53); the incidents pertaining to the birth of Parāśara (1.169) and his fathering of Vyāsa (1.57); the incarnation of the gods into the heroes of the Epic (1.61); the episode of Duśvanta and Śakuntalā (1.62-69) and the story of Yayāti who bestows his old age on Puru (1.70-83). Vyāsa became the natural grandfather of the Pāṇḍavas by begetting Pāṇḍu and Dhṛtarāṣṭra on their father's behalf. The remainder of the *Ādi-parva* follows the Sanskrit text fairly closely. Hazeu (1901) argues for a relation of the *Ādi-parva* with the *Bhāratamañjarī* by Kṣemendra.[53] Both omit twelve similar episodes. The incident of the house of gum is the same. The Pāṇḍavas meet Hidimbā. They meet Kṛṣṇa at Drupada's capital, marry Draupadī and move to Indraprastha. They help Agni burn down the Khāṇḍava forest. An example of an addition is, for instance, after *Mbhr.* 1.71.54, where Vaiśampāyana admonishes that Brahmans ought to abstain from drinking spirituous liquor. The Old Javanese adds *"daging ing celeng,"* i.e., "pork," a meat to which Islam objects.

The *Sabhā* and *Araṇyaka-parvas* are missing, but later literature shows that they were known. The *Virāṭa-parva* contains the incidents of the Pāṇḍavas adopting new names, hiding their arms under the guise of their mother's corpse and assuming menial professions, Kīcaka's infatuation and his subsequent murder and mutilation. Trigartas invade the Matsya country, but are repelled; Virāṭa's son, here called Bhumiñjaya, takes Bṛhannalā as charioteer, but the latter soon takes up arms and delivers a mighty battle with the Kauravas, while the gods Varuṇa and Kubera watch. He defeats the enemy and here the manuscript ends.

The *Udyoga-parva* has not many Sanskrit passages, and the ones surviving are corrupt. It covers the peace negotiations, Kṛṣṇa's departure to Dvāravatī where both parties solicit his help. Śalya first wishes to join the Pāṇḍavas, then reconsiders, but promises to betray Karṇa when steering his chariot. He justifies himself, as in the Sanskrit, by recounting the story of Indra killing Vṛtra treacherously. Nahuṣa's reign, his pride and fall, Vidura's counsel to Dhṛtarāṣṭra, as well as the Sanatsujāta passage are found here; Kṛṣṇa's address to the Kaurawa council is followed by an account of Kaṇva on Mātali and Garuḍa. Then Nārada tells the story of Viśvāmitra and Gālava. Then, to counteract a conspiracy, Kṛṣṇa shows himself in his divine form. The armies get ready and Uluka visits the Pāṇḍavas. Bhīṣma relates the story of Ambā and how he fought Paraśurāma.

The *Bhīṣma-parva* follows the Sanskrit text fairly closely. Kṛṣṇa tries to persuade Karṇa to join the Pāṇḍavas, but fails. The *Bhagavad-gītā* is recited. Many battle scenes are described, which are interrupted by the setting of the sun. Many episodes have been condensed and recast, some unknown incidents elaborated and a peculiar ending, whereby Bhīṣma utters a moral speech on kingship is very much like the *Rājadharma-parvan* of the Sanskrit. Śikhaṇḍin is here also the indirect cause of Bhīṣma's death, whereas Arjuna shoots him so full of arrows that when he tumbles from the chariot, head first, he does not touch the ground. A heavenly voice announces that he will not die until the *uttarāyaṇa,* the Southern position of the sun, which on Java, at least, does not make much sense.

Six books are missing and we continue with the *Āśramavasana-parva* which describes how Dhṛtarāṣṭra and Gāndhārī are treated very well at Yudhiṣṭhira's palace after the war, except by Bhīma who harbors a grudge and often bursts out in tears when he sees Yudhiṣṭhira pay homage to Dhṛtarāṣṭra. When he is alone with the old king he insults him: *"The scions of the sightless monarch by me with my arm like a bludgeon* . . .: 'Father Dhṛtarāṣṭra, you who are blind right down to your heart, look at my arms, which do not differ from the mace of the god of Death; then you will become sad about the destruction of your sons!' *'Slain are your kith and kin:'* Your relatives and sons have been butchered, without one remaining . . ."

The cursive print corresponds to the often corrupt Sanskrit, whereas the remainder is the Javanese paraphrase which is usually not very different.

Dhṛtarāṣṭra with Kuntī and Gāndhārī decides to leave for a hermitage. Before his departure, he gives Yudhiṣṭhira sage advice reminiscent of its original: "And you ought to act as follows: if it is hard to conquer the enemy, you should conclude a treaty etc. If he cannot be won by a treaty etc. *'may he go on an expedition accompanied by troops,'* then you should go forth to battle, then is the proper time . . ."

The Pāṇḍavas later visit their elders. Vidura expires leaning against a tree. Vyāsa entertains the living with a magic picture of the dead, but the latter do not mix with the living. Nor do the widows "dressed in white" throw themselves in the Ganges. After their return the brothers hear that the old people have perished in a forest fire, which is not stated to have been a sacrificial fire.

In the *Musala-parva* is the story of the provocation of the ṛṣis by a few youths. After some time, the god Kali descends in human form, black-faced, dark brown in hue, and hairless. Omens appear: "mice nibbled at (people's) nails and hair by night, swamp birds hooted like owls and sheep bleated like howling jackals; among animals donkeys mated with cows, young elephants with mares, tom cats with female ichneumons" (o.c., p. 126). The scene of the massacre is related in vivid detail. Kṛṣṇa dies as in the Epic and his sixteen thousand wives are taken to Indraprastha by Arjuna. A few commit suicide.

In the last *parva,* the *Prasthānika,* the Pāṇḍavas' *pradakṣiṇa* takes place which ends at the Sea of Sand, the *Vālukārṇṇava.* Here, unlike in the Sanskrit, Bhīma has to force his way into heaven and Karṇa approaches them to ask for reconciliation. Yudhiṣṭhira's episode with the dog who is Dharma, also occurs.

If the Old Javanese *Mahābhārata* is merely a "diluted abstract of the original written in a half childish, half homiletic style" in very prosaic language, the same cannot be said for the many works of literature which based themselves on the Epic. One of the earliest and most famous was the Old-Javanese *Bhārata-Yuddha* [54] "Battle of the Bhāratas" (early twelfth century) from the pen of two authors, Seḍah and Panuluh. Under the guise of presenting the Bhārata story, they apparently referred to the life-work of King Jayabhaya of Keḍiri to restore the unity of the Javanese realm. It is in simple, yet powerful, often poetic style and derives its incidents from the *Udyoga, Bhīṣma-, Droṇa-, Karṇa-,* and *Śalya-parvas.* The poem follows the *Mahābhārata* fairly closely. The story begins when Kṛṣṇa appears at Duryodhana's court to demand a partition of the country. The Kauravas reject his claims and to frustrate a plot he assumes his divine form as Viṣṇu with four arms, three heads and three eyes. After a visit to Kuntī, Kṛṣṇa returns to Virāṭa. The next morning the armies march out, and before the battle Kṛṣṇa admonishes Arjuna very briefly: he urges him to fight bravely, for it would be against the tradition that a *kṣatriya* would withdraw from the battle. Then the battle takes place in all its horror. Bhīṣma is slain, Bhagadatta, Abhimanyu follow, then Arjuna has a vision of Rudra who presents him with the Paśupati weapon on the eve of the thirteenth day of the battle. The next morning Kṛṣṇa and Arjuna proceed to the battlefield and strike terror into their enemies' hearts by blowing on their horns Devadatta and Pañcajanya.

The composers of the *Bhārata-Yuddha* were no mean poets. The work is full of attractive and novel similes, especially employing erotic imagery. When the sun rises, it is "red as the tired eyes of a loved one" (Canto V.1). When Arjuna's young son Abhimanyu is assailed from all sides, he decides to fight back to the very end.

> If one would now wish to describe his counter-assault, than he could be compared to a youth who for the first time throws himself in the arms of a girl. The flashing of sharp steel became identified with her frowning eyebrows. "Surely those must be women's nails," he thought, when his chest was wounded by arrows. So also he imagined the squeaking of the wagons, the trumpeting of elephants and the neighing of horses to be the moaning of a young woman (XIII. 29).

The Sanskrit *Mahābhārata* at the same place (7.48.6) compares him to a porcupine.

Besides this Old Javanese *Bhārata-Yuddha,* a New Javanese reworking exists composed at the court of Sultan Paku Buvânȧ III (1749-88). "Very unskilled in writing is His Majesty's servant, who at the order of his Highness undertakes the reworking of His Majesty's highly renowned poem, the excellent story that bears the name *Bràtȧ-yuda.*" [55] Thus begins this poem of sixty-nine cantos. It follows the text of the *Bhārata-Yuddha* quite closely. But whereas in the older poem Śikhaṇḍin was a hermaphrodite, a hero who assists Arjuna in slaying Bhīṣma, in the reworking he has become Arjuna's wife, Devi Sikandi. Bhīṣma's death is related as follows:

> The beautiful Devi Sikandi comes to receive instructions; the commands of King Krĕsna are requested by the Princess of Campala.—Rĕsi Bismȧ is terrified as he sees Sikandi approach. Fear grips the sage and he beckons King Yudiṣṭhira with the hand. The son of Darma, beseeched to save his (Bismȧ's) life, pretends ignorance and acts as if he does not perceive it. He lowers his eyes so that in effect he does not see it. He signals with his eyes to Sikandi to approach her brother the king and to go to battle; Arjuna

has to mount the chariot of the Princess of Campala.—Sikandi, at first secretly instructed by Sri Krĕsna, shoots an arrow which strikes the holy Bismå in the chest, but without injuring him. Immediately, Partå shoots a second arrow to drive the first one in. He hits it in the shaft and drives it fast into the breast; a jet of blood squirted from the wound and tumbling Bismå fell down in his chariot (16.22-17.1).

He was not quite dead yet, but died a few minutes later after Arjuna had given him water in which he had rinsed the arrows that struck Bhīṣma. In the remainder, one incident stands out, namely that Śalya when steering Karṇa's chariot, betrays him by pulling the reins when he is aiming an arrow at Arjuna. The chariot rears and the arrow lands in Arjuna's diadem not hurting him.[56] Then Arjuna finishes off Karṇa.

A Malayan version, *Hikayat Pāṇḍawa Djaya*[57] also exists. It probably goes back to an original that is now lost. Kĕsna upon his arrival at Astina as an emissary, is beleaguered by eager women who want to love him. Devi Sĕrikandi (Śikhaṇḍin) as in the New Javanese version is Arjuna's wife and follows him into battle. The *Bhagavadgītā* is found in a very brief form: when Arjuna expresses compassion for the enemy, Kĕsna irritatedly cuts him off with the remark that in the face of the enemy such language is inappropriate. The battle is described in gory detail. Bisma's death is like in the *Bhārata-Yuddha:* he is laid on a bed of arrows and Arjuna shoots a well into the ground from which water gushes forth to please Bisma. The names of the other Paṇḍavas are Darmavañsa (Yudhiṣṭhira), Bima, si Kula (Nakula), and Sadeva. Karṇa is often Ambakarna, Dhṛtarāṣṭra Dăstrāta. Arjuna at one point in the battle is killed, but Kĕsna revives him with a magic flower. Not Yudhiṣṭhira, but Bima shouts out loud that Droṇa's son Sotama (Aśvatthāman) has been killed. Kĕsna saves Arjuna from being struck by Karṇa's arrow by pushing the chariot down into the ground, so that it strikes his head ornament only. Salya had announced loudly when Karṇa was going to shoot his magic arrow. Arjuna becomes king of Astinapura.

The *Arjuna-vivāha*[58] "Arjuna's marriage" by Mpu Kanwa, is another Old Javanese reworking of an Epic story. It dates from Airlangga's reign and is composed in thirty-six cantos. It deals with Arjuna's penance on Mount Indrakila. He had accumulated so much power that the gods thought he might be fit to combat the demon king Nivākavaca for them. To test Arjuna, they dispatched a number of heavenly nymphs, among them Tilottamā and Suprabhā. In spite of their efforts at seduction, Arjuna remained unmoved. Indra then visits him in the guise of a sage who questioned him to test his philosophical acumen. Having passed that test, he is approached by a huge boar, a demon incarnate, whom Arjuna shoots dead. Then Śiva as a Kirāṭa visits him; they quarrel and fight, and finally Śiva reveals himself in his *Ardhanārīśvara* shape. Arjuna receives the Pāśupata weapon and after many incidents combats the demon Nivātakavaca and kills him with an arrow in his mouth. He becomes Lord of Heaven for seven days, frolicking with the nymphs. Then he returns to his brothers. The work has also been translated into New Javanese.[59]

Scenes from the *Arjuna-vivāha* have been carved on the third terrace of the Caṇḍi Jago,[60] a Hindu temple in Central Java dating from the middle of the thirteenth century. Arjuna and Śiva both are observing a boar with an arrow sticking in it. Other scenes are also shown. On an even older decoration inside a hermit's cave near Tuluñ Aguñ,[61] Arjuna is shown performing penance on Mount Indrakila. The nymphs descend from heaven and "thought they could conquer him with their temptations. . . They did not know, however, that the joy of sexual union is surpassed by (that of) complete meditation which triples the greatest joy . . . , like a stick made from the branch of a cocoanut palm (*savi*) (is surpassed in height) by a mountain. . . . The nymphs became infatuated. . . One began to whistle, smack her lips while cracking the knucles of her toes." Two nymphs stand outside while one remains to seduce him in earnest (*Arj. Viv.* III.8 and IV.2).

It is not possible, in this brief survey, to enumerate even in rough outline the numerous *wayang* "puppet-play" adaptations that exist of *Mahābhārata* stories.[62] The *Mahābhārata* incidents are often retold very freely. Arjuna is a lover with many affairs, Bhīma a superhumanly strong fighter, often the main hero of a bellicose story. Ekalaya in one story has his thumb amputated by Dorna (Droṇa) who transplants it to Arjuna's hand. Ekalaya's soul meets Ambā's and together they decide to be reborn as warriors on the Pāṇḍava side, as Notajunna (Dhṛṣṭadyumna) and Srikhandi (Śikhaṇḍin). In one late *lakon "wayang* story," the house of gum is used for a chess game between Duryodhana and Yudhiṣṭhira, but the bamboos used in its construction have been filled with gunpowder. The Pāṇḍavas are drugged except for Bhīma who rescues them all just before the house explodes with a terrible bang.[63] In the *Koravāśrama* the Kurus are revived and practice penance to avenge themselves.

Hindu influence in Java came to an end with the invasion of the Mohammedans in the fifteenth century. The Hindus were driven east, and many landed in Bali. It is here that Hinduism still exists and many of the old texts were found. In the eighteenth century a slow renaissance of Hindu culture began. The *Wayang* plays became popular again and derived many of their themes from mythological stories, being recited both in Malay and Javanese. Serrurier (1896, p. 219) gives a curious example of the Islamization of a *Mahābhārata* hero. According to an oral legend, Yudhiṣṭhira succumbs to the power of a Mohammedan *sjahādat* and was buried according to Islamic rites.

VIII *The* Mahābhārata *in Other Parts of Asia*

We can be brief about the influence of the *Mahābhārata* elsewhere in Asia. With China the Indians maintained an active commerce although it never became a colony. Buddhism swept China in the early centuries of our era, but with one sole exception, no records of *Mahābhārata* stories have ever been reported. The exception is the story of the Man in the Well whose oldest version we find in the *Mahābhārata,* although it has been widely adopted by Jains, Persians, Chinese, Japanese, and Christians.

In the Chinese version, the man is pursued by a mad elephant; he sees a well beside which is a tree with a vine growing from it. In the well are three venomous serpents watching for prey. Outside it are four other ones. A white and a black rat gnaw at the vine in the tree. Venomous bees sting the man, but now and again a drop of honey falls into his mouth. The man in his craving for honey is oblivious of his peril. The Chinese explanation is very elaborate. The rats, the serpents, the vine, the elephant, the well, the dragons inside it, the hand that clings to the vine, the honey are all endowed with special significance.[64]

West of India, in Iran and Arabia, equally little is known of the *Mahābhārata.* In the seventh and eighth centuries, many Sanskrit works were translated into Pahlavi, the language of Persia of that time. Most of these works have been lost, but some survive in Arabic translations. Among them is the *Mujmalū'-t-Tawarikh,*[65] a condensation of the *Mahābhārata.* It focuses on the geographical area of India that was then occupied by the Mohammedans. Duryodhana's sister

Duḥśalā, who is unimportant in the Sanskrit *Mahābhārata,* here is married to Jandrat (Jayadratha) and rules over the Sind. The Arabic translator repeatedly expresses his skepticism with regard to the veracity of our Epic. When recounting how Pāṇḍu's wives conceived their children through the intervention of the gods, he translates that they had intercourse with "the children of the Air" and adds: "The author (i.e., Vyāsa) tells the most ridiculous stories about this subject." In the end, Gāndhārī, struck by grief about the death of her one hundred sons, fasts and then stacks all the bodies in a large pile which she climbs to reach for food that she imagines is floating in the air. She finally burns them all.

The *Mahābhārata* was again translated into Persian under Akbar's regime (1556-1605) and was completed in 1585. It became known as the "Imperial Version," or the *Razm Nāma.* The emperor was motivated by the loftiest goals in ordering this translation: he desired that the "Mahābhārata, which is replete with most valuable things connected with religion, be translated so that those who display hostility may refrain from doing so and may seek the truth" (Harshe, p. 279). Akbar's idealism made him believe that the two great cultures under his rule might be united if they understood each other's philosophy. Four other translations followed this Imperial one. It seems to follow the Sanskrit rather closely.[66]

IX *The* Mahābhārata *in Antiquity and the Middle Ages*

The relationship between the ancient Greeks and the Indians has been the subject of many inquiries. Alexander's invasion of India in 325 B.C. extended the boundaries of the Hellenistic sphere of influence to Pakistan and North India. After Alexander's death the Greeks who had remained behind in India in time more or less assimilated with the native inhabitants. The opinions of the Brahmanical redactor of the *Mahābhārata* about the *Yavana's* is not flattering. To the conservative Hindu the Greeks' free way of life was apparently quite appalling. Śalya is from Madra, a country now in Pakistan, and at that time presumably occupied by Greeks. Karṇa when abusing Śalya (8.27.71-91) refers to his countrymen as wicked: all family members, men and women, eat together, consuming beef and rum (*sīdhu*) noisily and laughing. When intoxicated by rum, they dance. They also eat onions. A wise Brahman should not go there. We have reason to believe, however, that greater harmony existed between the invaders and the Hindus than the *Mahābhārata* suggests.[67]

Did the Greeks know the *Mahābhārata*? The Greeks in their motherland probably not, but there is some evidence that those living in India at least knew of it. A Prākrit inscription from the hand of Heliodorus, son of Diya (Dion) a Greek ambassador to some Suṅga king in the middle of the second century B.C., quotes a verse that bears striking similarity to a *Mahābhārata* Sanskrit stanza.[68] Heliodorus called himself a *Bhāgavata,* a confessor of the Bhāgavata faith of which Kṛṣṇa is the supreme being.

Two Greek warriors are said to have been incorporated in the *Mahābhārata,* Apollodotus, who appears as King Bhagadatta of the Yavanas and Demetrius who is identified with Dattamitra (*Mbhr.,* Calcutta edition, C.1. 5573). The former is mentioned several times fighting on the side of Duryodhana.[69] His capital is "Prāgjyotiṣa near the ocean," perhaps Bengal or Assam. Would the Greeks be there? The latter occurs in an interpolated passage from a northern manuscript (*Cr. Ed. App.* II, no. 80, line 45) and so is not properly part of our Epic anymore.

The Greek rhetorician Dio Chrysostomos, moreover, mentions that the Indians possessed and used a translation of Homer in their language.[70] It is probable that Dio referred to the *Mahābhārata,* a battle story that bears rough similarity to the *Iliad*. For the remainder, Greek records are silent on the topic of the *Mahābhārata*.

India's relations with Rome are hardly better reflected in the Epic. One disputed reference to Rome is found in the *Sabhā-parvan* where Sahadeva is said to have conquered Antioch and Rome, but the reading *romām* is uncertain, though quite likely correct.[71] It has also been suggested that the plot of the *Mahābhārata* was used by Virgil in the composition of his *Aeneid*.[72] There are some striking parallels between the two epics, too many to be credited to chance only. The last six books of the *Aeneid* deal with the battle between Aeneas, the Trojan invader, and Turnus, the crown-prince of Latium. The Trojan hero would correspond to a Pāṇḍu, especially Bhīma. Turnus resembles Duryodhana whereas Latinus, like old King Dhṛtarāṣṭra, is a ruler who is unable to impose his will.

The battle in both epics lasts 18 days. This agreement is one of the strongest pieces of evidence. The exchange of delegates to plead for peace in Book five of the *Mahābhārata* and Book seven of the *Aeneid,* in both cases fails in spite of efforts of Dhṛtarāṣṭra and

Latinus to save the peace. There is a nocturnal battle in both epics (*Mbhr.* 10; *Aeneid,* X). Mars assists the Trojans very much like Kṛṣṇa assists the Pāṇḍavas. As in the *Mahābhārata,* Virgil ends three of his books (X, XI, XII) with the death of a general. Most of these features are not taken over from Virgil's other source of inspiration, Homer's *Iliad*. We do not know how or when Virgil might have heard the *Mahābhārata*. An active commerce existed between Egypt and India in the days of the Roman empire and it is not unlikely that bards accompanied the caravans. Virgil himself visited Egypt for six months after the summer of A.D. 29.[73] His work would mark the earliest independent attestation of the *Mahābhārata* plot.

The transmission of Indian stories to the West is more definitely established by another series of narratives, the *Pañcatantra*. It is a set of animal fables with a history of translation and borrowing from the Indian source to the modern English via Pahlavī, Arabic, Hebrew, Greek, and Latin.

The literature of the Middle Ages in Europe contains one story that originated in the *Mahābhārata*. John of Damascus (eighth century) composed a set of fables which included the story of the Man in the Well, which he had based on a set of legends describing the life of the Buddha. The work, under the name of *Barlaam and Josaphat*[74] was translated into Latin A.D. 1048-49. By the early thirteenth century it had found its way into the *Gesta Romanorum* where the story of the Man in the Well appears as Chapter 168, "On Eternal Damnation:"[75]

> Barlaam narrates that a sinner resembles a certain man who when afraid of a unicorn, stepped backwards into a pit; but when he had fallen he seized with his hands a little bush which was growing up from the depth and looking down, he saw at the bottom of the tree a very black well and a horrible dragon coiled around the tree and waiting for his fall with the mouth open. Moreover, as two mice, one white, the other black, were continuously gnawing the root, he felt it sway. Also, four white vipers moving forth from the place where he had fixed his foot, poisoned the air with their fatal breath. Lifting up his eyes, he saw a flow of honey dripping from the branches of the tree and forgetting the peril in which he had been placed on all sides, he gave himself up completely to that sweetness. Then, when a certain friend passed him a ladder, he tarried and as the tree broke, fell into the mouth of the dragon. The latter went down into the well and devoured him there and so he died, alas, a miserable death.

The moral of the story is expounded as follows: the unicorn

(who was an elephant in the Indian story) is Death, the pit is this life, the white and black mouse are day and night, the four vipers are the four humors of the body which is the tree; the dragon is the devil, the well on the bottom is hell; the sweetness of the honey is the delight in sinning tempting the human being; the friend is Christ, the ladder penitence which if refused leads to a precipitous fall into the Devil's mouth.

The purpose of the story has certainly undergone some changes, more than the details in fact. From Vidura's attempt to console old Dhṛtarāṣṭra and set him at peace with the world, it has been transformed into an eloquent admonition from the Church Militant to abide by its doctrines of salvation. The story has been rendered into a bas-relief by the thirteenth-century Italian sculptor Benedetto Antelami, or one of his pupils, on the Porta della Vita (1260-62) of the Battistero in Parma.[76] Claims that Dante borrowed it for the first scene of his *Commedia* can be discounted.[77]

Through the agency of Christian missionaries, the story reached Japan in the sixteenth century. It seems to be the only and very remote connection of that country with the *Mahābhārata*.[78]

As late as the nineteenth century, this episode in a Russian translation from the Georgian version, exerted a powerful influence on the thinking of the youthful Leo Tolstoy and contributed to his resolve to lead an unconventional life.[79]

CHAPTER 7

The Mahābhārata *Since the Eighteenth Century*

AFTER the Middle Ages,[1] we find the *Bhagavad-gītā* emerging in the West as the first Sanskrit work to be translated when Charles Wilkins' English translation appeared in 1785. Ten years later it was followed by the Śakuntalā episode. Kālidāsa's *Śakuntalā* found great favor with the German poet Goethe. The Nala episode was first edited under the name *Nalus* by Franz Bopp (1819), and its simple Sanskrit has since made it a favorite text in introductory Sanskrit readers. Together with the Sāvitrī episode, it has inspired some German and English authors to compose elegiac ballads or prose works which rarely convey the simple, earnest and devout tone of the original.[2] The Śakuntalā story that is usually found in Western editions, is not the *Mahābhārata* story, but Kālidāsa's masterpiece. Even a musical overture from the hand of the Hungarian composer Karl Goldmark was named *Śakuntalā,* and was first performed in 1865. For translations and adaptations of the *Mahābhārata,* see the section on bibliography.

By far the best-known part of the *Mahābhārata,* however, is the *Bhagavad-gītā.* Its translations are too numerous to list and they vary in quality. More than any other Indian literary work, it has become a medium for communicating to the outside world the essence of Indian speculative thought. Religious movements with an Oriental flavor, such as theosophy and Sufism, draw on the *Bhagavad-gītā* as a source of inspiration. During the Emerson-Thoreau period of Concord, Mass., the teachings of the *Bhagavad-gītā,* according to one investigator, have been operative as an enzyme. Also Wm. T. Harris' thought and the St. Louis movement of nineteenth-century America, seem to have undergone its influence.[3] Western authors such as Jean Herbert use it, as well as other parts of the *Mahābhārata,* as a vehicle for expressing their mystic convictions. They often do violence to the text to suit their arguments.[4] It is clear that together with the *Upaniṣads*—which through the intermediary of several translations exerted a great influence on the nineteenth-century German philosopher Schopenhauer—and a few classical dramas, as well as the epic episodes described earlier, the *Bhagavad-gītā* has become the major contribution of Sanskrit literature to world literature.

Returning to India now, we shall try and assess the role the *Mahābhārata* has been playing in this age of change. Necessarily, this survey can be very general only. It is about as difficult as it would be to estimate the importance of the Homeric epics to modern Greece. In both cases, the tradition has been interrupted by a period of Islamic rule although the ties binding the present-day Indian to his past are avowedly much stronger. The extent of the Epic's influence on India cannot be estimated with any degree of certitude, yet should be considered. Indian authors when discussing the subject rarely advance beyond statements such as "To trace the influence of the epic . . . is to comprehend the real history of the people during the 3000 years" and "the content of our collective unconscious wherein breathes the united soul of India." [5] Perhaps that it all that can be said.

Some works of art remain that portray scenes from the *Mahābhārata,* but on the whole surprisingly few good works are extant. One famous representation of the Pāṇḍavas is found in the Gupta temple of Deogarh, Orissa, dating from A.D. 600.[6] The five Pāṇḍava brothers and Draupadī are represented near Viṣṇu lying on a snake. Bhīma carries a mace. Another Gupta bas-relief shows Arjuna performing penance. At Māmmalapuram in South India a number of small temples (*rathas*) dating from the Pallava dynasty (600-850) are named after Draupadī, Arjuna, Bhīma, Dharmarāja, and Sahadeva, for no apparent reason. The temple named Draupadī, for instance, is dedicated to the goddess Kāli. But also at Māmmalapuram is the most famous relief showing the descent of the Ganges on the head of Śiva, which is also called "Arjuna's penance." But that it really refers to Arjuna's self-imposed torture on the Himālayas, is doubtful.[7]

In addition, numerous smaller sculptures, icons, and devotional pictures are said to exist, most commonly showing Arjuna on a chariot absorbing wisdom from Kṛṣṇa. But these pictures must be seen against the background of devotionalism which spread later in India. The Kurus are never honored with representations. The dearth of significant works of art inspired by the *Mahābhārata* is not easy to explain. One would imagine that the mighty weapon feats of Arjuna, the great sacrifices of King Yudhiṣṭhira, the battle between good and evil nations, the conventions of wise people in remote hermitages would lend proper pious themes for a work of art. Java and Cambodia excel over India in this respect. Perhaps the Mohammedan invaders destroyed some.

In the eighteenth century, the Persian translation of the *Mahābhārata,* the *Razm-Nāma,* was often profusely illustrated with miniatures of great beauty. One shows Damayantī's *svayaṃvara* where she sits in a palanquin, unveiled, putting a garland around the neck of Nala who is dressed in medieval Indian costume.[8] The modern painter George Keyt has depicted the combat of Bhīma and Jarāsaṃdha in a painting.[9] Literature provides us with one scale with which to gauge the influence of this Epic that for such a long period has been with the Indian people. But two events of great significance divide the modern Indian from Epic man. One is the Islam invasion and its dominance for many centuries; another is the emergence of the Bhakti movement that arose in opposition to Islam and swept India from shore to shore. The Islam, as well as its offspring, the Sikh movement, is still quite active in India, and both disavow any debt to Hindu scriptures.

Favorite Bhakti heroes were Kṛṣṇa and Rāma. The former is worshipped in a variety of forms, mostly taken from the *Purāṇas,* not from the *Mahābhārata.* Our Epic did not lend itself very easily to devotional characterization; even so, devotees succeeded in abstracting a few sories in which the warrior Kṛṣṇa acts as the beneficent savior. In Sūr Dās's *Sūr Sāgar,*[10] for instance, the episode of Draupadī's disrobement is reworked into an impassioned entreaty of the devotee Draupadī to Kṛṣṇa, to save her from her plight. Jarāsaṃdha's prisoners, as in the *Purāṇas,* express their deep gratitude to Kṛṣṇa, rather than to Bhīma who had been responsible for the king's death. Kṛṣṇa appears as Arjuna's charioteer, riding on and with a mighty roar protecting Arjuna from the flames and anguish of the battlefield by his divine strength. In devotional art, also many similar adaptations of *Mahābhārata* stories can be found. The *Mahābhārata* Kṛṣṇa is not distinguished from the sensual love hero of the *Bhāgavata-purāna* and so we find scenes of an erotic Kṛṣṇa alternating with Epic incidents.

Most modern vernacular works exist in the native languages only. A few have been translated and we shall examine some of them here.

The Bengali poet Rabindranath Tagore (1861-1941) adopted several incidents from the *Mahābhārata* as themes for his dramas. Among them are *Chitra,* inspired by the Śakuntalā story, *Gāndhārī's prayer* and the dialogue of *Karṇa and Kuntī:* [11] In the last play, Karṇa meets Kuntī without knowing who she is, but she knows he is her son. He senses some mysterious alliance with her, but ashamed as she is for having abandoned him, she does not reveal at first her purpose, *viz.,* to make amends. When he finds out that she is his mother and angrily asks why she had "set a bottomless chasm between Arjuna and himself," she tearfully exclaims: ". . . to-day your recreant mother implores you for generous words. Let your forgiveness burn her heart like fire and consume its sin." Karṇa replies: "Mother, accept my tears!" and all ends happily.

Modern authors writing in English also occasionally use *Mahābhārata* themes. Vasudeva Rao in 1928 wrote a play called *Nala and Damayantī* [12] in blank verse wherein the two lovers appear much like Romeo and Juliet in an Oriental garden. When sued by Nala and the gods, Damayantī exclaims to Nala:

> Ah me vex not a heart that yearns for thy love.
> But mortal maid am I; how may I wed
> The Gods? Each life has its own element;
> The fish takes to the salt wave of the brine,
> But die it must if cast into a sea
> Which flows with milk, if that were possible.
> I love thee, Nala . . .

The South Indian poet T. P. Kailasam wrote, among others, two plays inspired by Epic themes, but interpreted in a modern way. *Fulfillment* [13] deals with the incident of Ekalavya (1.123), Droṇa's pupil, who here had decided to join the Kurus on the eve of the battle. Kṛṣṇa attempts to dissuade him in a lengthy, sophist harangue, but to no avail; Ekalavya is bitter about Arjuna's wicked deed. So Kṛṣṇa kills Ekalavya treacherously, promising the dying outcast that his mother will not be made to grieve. Then Kṛṣṇa proceeds to kill Ekalavya's mother too. In *Karṇa, the Brahman's Curse,* Kailasam portrays Karṇa as a Greek tragic hero who in spite of all his efforts fails to extricate himself from the web of fate in which he is caught. This interpretation is reminiscent of Bhāsa's (see p. 90).

The religious leader Sri Aurobindo Ghose composed a monumental ballad called *Sāvitrī*[14] in blank verse. It is inspired undoubtedly by the sweet little episode in the *Mahābhārata,* but has gained tremendously in volume. The poet took fifty years to write it. The story is told in twenty-four thousand lines of blank verse describing Sāvitrī's experiences on a symbolic as well as a physical level, with all the appropriate symbolic *double-entendre* designed to evoke the proper associations in the sympathetic reader. Book eight is called *Book of Death.* Here Sāvitrī and Satyavan joyously set out to chop wood. But as he swings the ax, the Great Woodsman takes a swing at him . . .

> . . . and his labour ceased: lifting
> His arm he flung away his poignant axe
> Far from him like an instrument of pain.
> She came to him in silent anguish and clasped,
> And he cried to her, "Savitri, a pang
> Cleaves through my head and breast . . ." (p. 200).

It takes another twenty-five lines before he cries out:

> Savitri, Savitri, O Savitri,
> Lean down, my soul, and kiss me while I die
> And even as her pallid lips pressed his,
> His failed, losing last sweetness of response.

Sāvitrī (=the Soul) then goes out on a long Journey (=Life) to meet Darkness (=Spiritual Blindness) and struggles to regain her beloved Satyavat (=Truth). And so the narrative moves on, relentlessly. These examples can only illustrate a few of the literary works in which the *Mahābhārata* has played a role.

In the vernacular literature throughout India, themes and personages of the *Mahābhārata* are used in hundreds of publications, books, dramas, popular plays, and festivals. In elementary schools, stories from the *Mahābhārata* are often retold with an appropriate moral. For example, in a Grade Three Reader, we find that from the *Mahābhārata* we can learn brother-love, such as is found among the Pāṇḍavas. The latter were fair and honest and thus were victorious over the crafty and cunning Kauravas. "Like the Pāṇḍavas, you must be honest and fair in your dealings."

The movies have also taken hold of the *Mahābhārata* and are milking one precious episode after another from the inexhaustible wishing cow of our Epic.[15]

If we wish to study the social influence of the *Mahābhārata* on Indian life of today, we have to enter into a vague, ill-defined area of social relations, customs, attitudes, and beliefs that can better be assessed by sociologists, psychologists, and anthropologists. It varies greatly from one part of India to the next. Any resemblances we may discover between the social structure of today and the moral prescriptions laid down in our Epic, are, from a purely descriptive point of view, of secondary importance. On the whole, an Indian of today models his behavior more according to the ethics prescribed in Tulsidās's *Rāmāyaṇa* than to those of the *Mahābhārata*. For instance, the notion of strength through self-control, *dama,* of meekness, submissiveness, and passive resistance are all traceable to this medieval work and only indirectly to the *Mahābhārata*. We do read in the Epic that *ahiṃsā* is the greatest virtue, but it was not a concept that the warrior of the *Mahābhārata* was guided by: killing people and animals, eating meat, and violence were practices he took for granted.

The term *ahiṃsā* is but seldom used in the *Mahābhārata*. A virtuous bird-catcher justifies his profession by stating: "Walking about all the time, (all) men with their feet kill many living creatures which are sitting on the ground . . . I say that, for *ahiṃsā* was ordained (as a virtue) by ignorant people in former days. Who, I wonder, does not injure creatures in this world, O best of twiceborn?" (3.199.25-28). He continues to say that absolute abstinence from injury is impossible, but there may be degrees of success in achieving the goal. Elsewhere in the Epic other terms are used: *adroha* "absence of malice" is listed with truthfulness and freedom from enmity among the chief virtues for all creatures (15.35.9). With truth, liberality and other virtues, *adroha* is listed as an eternal duty (12.60.7-8). When Yudhiṣṭhira during his interview with the Yakṣa proclaims the highest duty of man, he uses not the term *ahiṃsā,* but *ānṛśaṃsya-* "absence of cruelty" (3.297.71f.). By and large, the concept is a negative one: abstaining from injuring living creatures, and throughout the early ethical history of India, that is its exclusive meaning.

The statesman Mohandas K. Gandhi (rightly or wrongly) adopted the concept of *ahiṃsā* as one of the foundations of his political philosophy of passive resistance. He conceived of it in a more comprehensive manner than the early Sanskrit works, interpreting it to include the notion that it is good to be tolerant of one's fellow men, regardless of their wicked actions or intentions. This almost imperceptible extension of the meaning of *ahiṃsā,* transforms the ancient non-injury concept into a positive one, that of overcoming evil by personal suffering. Gandhi was deeply influenced by the *Bhagavad-gītā,* and his political philosophy has found widespread acceptance among the people of India and the rest of the world. As such, the *Mahābhārata*'s world outlook is still alive and remembered as an active principle in the political thinking of the twentieth century. Similarly in India, Sāvitrī and Damayantī still illustrate the ideal of the Hindu wife who submissively and devotedly regards her husband's happiness as her greatest joy.

Matters of customs and beliefs can be assessed only if one can rely on studies made by competent field workers. Not enough work has been done to make even a general evaluation. H. Bachmann [16] thinks that many different peoples of India possess a fundamental common ethical trait attributable to the ancient moral doctrines. How far and whether this statement is true, is arguable. If so, it is likely to be true for high-caste Hindus rather than for other groups. G. M. Carstairs [17] writes that high-caste Hindus believe that another person may be endowed with supernatural qualities which may be benevolent or not. Such a person could be a saint or a witch and if saintly, he is entitled to worship, much in line with the prescription in the *Mahābhārata:* "Such a person should be worshipped quietly" (5.43.34).

Many of the superstitions and magic practices described in Chapter 4 are still found in one part or another of India. For instance, Carstairs remarks that a Hindu man will regard his wife as a lustful creature always intent on robbing him of his power. This image is reflected in the *Mahābhārata* story of Svāhā, a female in love with the god Agni who disguised herself six times to sleep with him and rob him of his seed from which she created monsters (*Mbhr*. 3.214). But even such correspondences need not imply a necessary connection between Epic teaching and local practices.

In a study of high school students in the northeastern part of Madhya Pradesh, McGavran tested the belief in traditional values of the boys. He found (Table IV) that more than 50 percent of the Hindu students still believed in the sanctity of the ancient books, including the *Mahābhārata*. They rated this belief at a par with the belief in a personal, yet universal deity, in the holiness of the cow and in the superiority of Brahmans.[19]

Present-day Indian statesmen, thinkers, and religious leaders naturally derive their ideas from a variety of sources, many of which are Western, and many Indian. Mohandas Gandhi, Jawaharlal Nehru, and Vivekananda were educated in English schools; their ethnic background allowed them to reinterpret in terms understandable to the West that which was appealing and expedient in their own culture. To trace back any of their ideas to a work like the *Mahābhārata* would require a special and perhaps rewarding study. Another philosopher, Dr. Kurtkoti,[20] has attempted to put the *Bhagavad-gītā* in the perspective of the problem of political and social equality, but has to resort to rather drastic reinterpretations. The keynote of the *Bhagavad-gītā,* he states, is *samatva* "equanimity." It "advocates freedom and prescribes force only as the last recourse. If then, the richer classes or individuals . . . do their duty properly . . . there is some justification for the learned man, the soldier, the politician, the merchant, the lawyer . . . having some privilege, some position, some preferential treatment in material comforts; for by their conduct they show that they are entitled to this sort of privilege and protection" (p. 4). "But in my opinion you have only to run to the *Mahābhārata* for the purest light and the most helpful guide to be had for the solution of these (social and economic) problems . . ." (ib., p. 4).

Summary

LOOKING back on the history of the *Mahābhārata* in relation to the art, literature, and thinking of the world, we can distinguish at least two main spheres in which it has been influential. The first is the sphere of entertainment and escape literature. Authors writing in Sanskrit, in modern Aryan and Dravidian languages, as well as in Javanese, English, French, and German have used the heroic story or the episodes for themes of plays, poems, novels, and romances. Both Pampa in Andhra Pradesh and Mpu Kanva in Java sought to glorify their patron kings by composing poems based on the *Mahābhārata.* In both cases the king became identified with the hero Arjuna. In Java especially, the *Mahābhārata* was regarded as a poem full of entertaining episodes and gory battles which lent themselves superlatively to entertain the population. The Old Javanese *Bhārata-Yuddha* is one of the finest heroic poems inspired by the *Mahābhārata.* Its composers, Panuluh and Seḍah, were poets of great imagination and perceptiveness. At the same time that Sanskrit authors in India were weaving worn-out clichés into their contrived, poetic fabrications, Panuluh and Seḍah found in their luxuriant, lively environment an abundance of fresh imagery, which replaced and often improved upon the stately, solemn Sanskrit hyperboles.

Similarly in Cambodia we find the exploits of King Jayavarman VII reflected in the reliefs he had carved around his palaces and temples and which were equated with *Mahābhārata* stories. But in India proper, the character of the *Mahābhārata* changes. True, we find traces of its heroic and entertaining aspects in the popular literature and perhaps the festivals, but by and large it has been turned into a religious work.

And this brings us to the other sphere of influence of the *Mahābhārata*. It has been and still is significant as a moral, philosophical, and religious work. The descent of God Viṣṇu who took flesh as Lord Kṛṣṇa and propounded the wisdom of the *Bhagavad-gītā* is a notion which the Hindu will associate more readily with the *Mahābhārata,* than its episodic narrative. The *Mahābhārata* is regarded as a religious work, hallowed by tradition, on a par with *Purāṇas* and the Lawbooks. We have seen that this notion existed already in Kumārila's work of the seventh century. Hindus today, steeped in a religion which values a personal god, attach much significance to the *Bhagavad-gītā* where a path to salvation by devotion is outlined. But they are not alone. Alberūni, the Arabic geographer, was impressed by the *Bhagavad-gītā* (see Winternitz, 1963, p. 375) and so were many Westerners of the previous century. Its advocacy of the doctrine of non-injury has been transformed with great success into a political doctrine of passive resistance.

In this light, it is not incorrect to conclude that east of India the *Mahābhārata* was influential and appreciated as a heroic poem and west of India as a carrier of spiritual wisdom through the agency of the *Bhagavad-gītā,* one of the most eloquent and profound statements found anywhere in the world about man's relationship to God.

Notes and References

Chapter One

1. Bowra, for example, does not regard the *Mahābhārata* as a heroic poem, because of the overburden of "literary and theological matter"; see H. M. Bowra, *Heroic Poetry* (London: MacMillan and Co., 1961), p. v.

2. Thus Maurice Winternitz, *History of Indian Literature* trans. from the German by S. Ketkar and rev. by the author, 2nd ed. (Calcutta: Univ. of Calcutta, 1963), p. 286.

3. *The Mahābhārata,* ed. Vishnu S. Sukthankar and others, 19 vols. (Poona: Bhandarkar Oriental Research Institute, 1929-66). Hereafter cited as *Mbhr.*

4. See Arthur A. Macdonell and Arthur Berriedale Keith, *Vedic Index* (London: John Murray, 1912), vol. 2 *s.v.*

Chapter Two

1. The figures in brackets refer to book, chapter and verse, respective of the *Mahābhārata.*

2. *Niṣādas* were a despised, low-ranking people.

3. A *Śvayaṃvara* is a typically Epic form of marriage, unknown before and after the heroic period. The bride has all the suitors introduced to her and chooses one, or else they engage in a contest whose winner receives the girl's hand. See Edward Washburn Hopkins, "The Social and Military Position of the Ruling Caste in Ancient India as Respresented by the Sanskrit Epic," *J.Am.Or.Soc.,* 13 (1889), 57-376.

4. The length of a *yojana* is unknown. Estimates vary from 2½ miles to seven or eight miles. See Pandurang V. Kane *History of Dharmaśāstra* (Poona; Bhandarkar Or. Res. Inst., 1953), Vol. IV, p. 628.

5. The dice, called *akṣa* were not of the type we know. The game

consisted of each opponent in turn taking a handful from a pile of dried fruit of the *vibhītaka* tree. The player scored if he had drawn a multiple of four. Larger, rectangular dice were also known. See Heinrich Lüders, "Das Würfelspiel im alten Indien," in *Philologica Indica* (Göttingen, 1940), pp. 106-74, and K. de Vreese, "The Game of Dice in Ancient India," in *Orientalia Neerlandica* (Leiden: Sijthoff, 1948), 349-62.

6. Two warriors named Rāma appear in the *Mahābhārata*. Most prominent is Jamadagni's son, later called *Paraśurāma* "Rāma with the axe"; the other is Daśaratha's son, the hero of the Rāma episode and of Vālmīki's *Rāmāyaṇa*.

7. That the *Rāmopākhyāna,* or Rāma *episode* is based on Vālmīki's great epic, has been proved conclusively by Sukthankar, "The Rāma Episode and the Rāmāyana," in *A Volume of Indological Studies Presented to Prof. P. K. Kane* (Poona: Bhandarkar Or. Res. Inst., 1941), 472-87.

8. The Indian notions about dreams have been discussed by E. Abegg, "Indische Traumtheorie und Traumdeutung," *Zeitschrift der Schweizerischen Gesellschaft für Asienkunde,* 12 (1960), 5-34.

9. To perform a horse sacrifice, the future monarch consecrated a horse which was left to roam free at will. It was followed by a strong detachment of the king's army who protected the horse as it wandered from country to country. Kings opposing the invasion had to deliver battle and, if defeated, were required to pay tribute to the king at the sacrificial festival. At the end of a year the horse was taken back to the capital and sacrificed according to Vedic rites.

10. This type of oath is very common in the Epic. The swearer states: "As surely as such and such about my own character is true, on the strength of that truth, let so and so happen." See E. Washburn Hopkins, "The Oath in Hindu Epic Literature," *JAOS,* 52 (1932), 316-37; Miles Dillon "The Hindu act of truth in Celtic tradition," *Mod. Philology* XLIV (1947) 137ff.

11. J. Darmesteter, "Points de contact entre le Mahābhārata et le Shah-Nāmah," *Journal Asiatique* 8th Series, Vol. X (1887), 38-75, believes that this episode was borrowed from Persian literature, *viz.,* from a prototype of the story of Kai Koshru's death, *Shah-Nāmah* XIII, end.

Chapter Three

1. See *Pānini's Grammatik* ed. Otto Böhtlingk (Leipzig, 1887), p. 315, *sūtra* 6.2.38. His date has been discussed in V. S. Agrawala, *India as known to Pānini* (Benares: Munshi Ram Manohar Lal,

1963), 2nd Rev. ed., Ch. VIII, with references to many previous theories.

2. See Adolf Holtzmann, *Das Mahābhārata und seine Theile* (Kiel, 1892-95), 4 vols.

3. See Joseph Dahlmann, S. J., *Das Mahābhārata als Epos und Rechtsbuch* (Berlin, 1895), 2 vols.

4. See Sylvain Lévi, "Tato jayam udīrayet," in *R. G. Bhandarkar Comm. Vol.* (Poona: Bhandarkar Or. Res. Inst., 1917), 99-106; English translation in *ABORI* 1 (1918), 13-20.

5. See E. Washburn Hopkins, *The Great Epic of India* (New York: Charles Scribner's Sons, 1902), pp. 386-402. The work will be cited hereafter as *GEI*.

6. See V. S. Sukthankar, *On the Meaning of the Mahābhārata* (Bombay: Asiatic Society, 1957), pp. 61-90. His views had been anticipated in part by Vittore Pisani, "The rise of the Mahābhārata," in *A volume of Eastern and Indian Studies Presented to Prof. F. W. Thomas* (Bombay, 1939), pp. 166-76.

7. See Nicolaus Mironow, *Die Dharmaparīkṣā des Amitagati* (Leipzig Dissertation, 1903), p. 52.

8. *manvādi bhāratam kecid āstīkādi tathā pare tatho 'paricarādy anye viprāḥ samyag adhīyate* (1.1.50).

9. A condensed genealogical table is given on p. xi.

10. The law of primogeniture is not stated explicitly, but can be inferred from the genealogical tables. A few times it is violated; see Iravati Karve, "Kinship Terms and Family Organization as Found in the Critical Edition of the Mahābhārata," *Bull. of the Deccan College Research Institute* (BDCRI) V (1943-44), pp. 61-148.

11. See above, note 6.

12. The figure 18 is prominent in Indian literature. There are 18 *Purāṇas,* our battle lasts 18 days, eighteen armies engage in the battle, and the *Bhagavad-gītā* has 18 chapters.

13. See V. S. Sukthankar, "The Parvasaṃgraha Figures," *ABORI* 23 (1930), pp. 549-58, and M. V. Vaidya, "The Extent of the Mahābhārata," in *Principal Karmarkar Comm. Vol.* (Poona, 1948), pp. 222-28.

14. See V. S. Sukthankar, "The Oldest Extant MS. of the Ādiparvan," *ABORI* 19 (1938), pp. 201-62. The manuscript is on birch bark.

15. See Franklin Edgerton, "The Epic Triṣṭubh and Its Hypermetric Varieties," *JAOS* 59 (1939), pp. 159-74, and especially Hopkins *GEI,* Chapter Four and Appendixes B and C, for a very complete description of *Mahābhārata* metrics. Many of the unusual varieties of meter have been rejected by the Critical Edition. An

example for the scansion of a *śloka* is the following verse (1.2.236):

śrutvā tv idam upākhyānam śrāvyam anyan na rocate
pumskokilarutaṃ śrutvā rūkṣa dhvāṅkṣasya vāg iva

"But having heard this story, one takes no delight in any other story worth hearing,
Just as he who has heard the call of the Indian cuckoo will think the crow's call harsh."

It is scanned as follows:

Syll. Nr.

1	2	3	4	5	6	7	8	1	2	3	4	5	6	7	8
–	–	v	v	v	–	–	–/	–	v	–	–	v	–	v	–
–	–	v	v	v	–	–	–/	–	–	–	–	v	–	v	v

An example of a *triṣṭubh* is the following verse (6.33.47):

mayā prasannena tavā' rjune' daṃ rūpaṃ paraṃ darśitam ātmayogāt,
tejomayaṃ viśvam anantam ādyam, yan me tvadanyena na dṛṣṭapūrvam

"By me, kindly disposed to you, O Arjuna, by my own power, this highest form has been shown,
That is made of splendor, universal, endless, excellent, that has not been seen by any one else but you before, of me."

16. Among noteworthy papers dealing with *Mahābhārata* grammar are the following: Susil K. De, "A Note on Hiatus in Epic Sandhi," *Indian Linguistics* 18 (1958), pp. 12-15; Franklin Edgerton, "Epic Studies," *BDCRI* 5 (1944), pp. 1-12; V. D. Gokhale, "Unpāninian Forms and Usages in the Critical Edition of the *Mahābhārata,* Compounds," *Indian Linguistics* 17 (1957), pp. 121-28; N. L. S. Gupta, "Studies in Epic Grammatical Forms," *Dacca University Studies* 3, No. 1 (1937), pp. 68-103; E. D. Kulkarni "Unpāninian Forms and Usages in the Critical Edition of the Mahābhārata," *BDCRI* 4 (1943), 227-45, *BDCRI* 5 (1944), 13-34, *BDCRI* 11 (1950), pp. 361-78, *NIA* 6 (1943), 130-39; M. A. Mehendale "Absolutives in the Critical Edition of the Virāṭaparvan," *BDCRI* 1 (1939), pp. 71-73.

17. R. K. Sharma, *Elements of Poetry in the Mahābhārata* (Berkeley: University of California Press, 1964), presents a detailed account of similes and other style figures in four of the books of the *Mahābhārata.*

18. George Dumézil, "La Transposition des dieux souverains mineurs en héros dans le Mahābhārata," *Indo-Iranian Journal* III,

No. 1 (1959), pp. 1-16, views the story of the three sons of Kuntī and their twin brothers as a variant of an ancient Indo-European myth.

19. See the literature quoted by A. D. Pusalker, *Studies in the Epics and Purāṇas* (Bombay: Bhavan's Book University, Bharatiya Vidya Bhavan, 1963), 2nd ed., pp. 145-46.

20. See Hopkins, "The Epic View of the Earth," *J. of the International School of Vedic and Allied Research* I, No. 2 (1930), pp. 68-87, for a reliable account of the boundaries of Epic India.

21. See *Viṣṇu-Purāna* 4.21.7. In the translation of Horace H. Wilson, *The Vishńu Puráṇa. . . .* ed. Fitzedward Hall (Calcutta: Punthi Pustak, 1964), 3d ed., it is on p. 451.

22. See Hopkins, "Ruling Caste. . ." (See Chapter 2, note 3), which contains a wealth of information on Epic institutions.

23. R. S. Sharma, *Śūdras in Ancient India* (Delhi: Motilal Banarsi Dass, 1958), has made a special study of the Śūdras and believes they were not slaves.

Chapter Four

1. For a discussion of these topics, see Chapter 5.

2. The mythology of the Epic has been described exhaustively by E. W. Hopkins, *Epic Mythology,* Grundriss der Indo-Arischen Philogie und Altertumskunde III; 1 B (Strassburg: Karl J. Trübner, 1915).

3. See also Charles Autran, *L'Épopée indoue* (Paris: Les Éditions Deno ¨1, 1946), pp. 66-169.

4. See E. Washburn Hopkins, "Magic Observances in the Hindu Epic," *Proc. Am. Philosoph. Soc.* 49 (1910), 24-40, who gives an account of these magical practices with references to the text.

5. See H. D. Sankalia, "Iconographical Elements in the Adiparva," *BDCRI* 5 (1943-44), pp. 149-61.

6. See Hopkins, *Epic Mythology,* p. 231.

7. Pusalker, *op. cit.,* pp. 84-111, reviews the theories proposed about the Kṛṣṇa figure. He argues for a non-composite, human, historical Kṛṣṇa.

Chapter Five

1. See for instance, *Mbhr.* 3.187.7ff., which shows how morality has decayed under the law of Karma; also 3.247.35 and 3.200. Examples of the retribution of acts in another life are given in 13.112. 32ff.

2. On *saṃsāra,* see for instance *Mbhr.* 14.16.30ff. and *Bhgg.* 14.14-20; also, G. Czerny, *Die Seelenwanderung im Mahābhārata*

(Tübingen, 1927), who raises the point that a person may be cursed to be reborn as a lower being.

3. For instance, *Mbhr.* 3.182-90; 5.6.1-3; 5.37-38; 12.329ff.

4. See Maurice Winternitz, "Asceticism in Ancient India," in *Some Problems of Indian Literature* (Calcutta, 1925), pp. 21-40. The *Mahābhārata* condemns false ascetics (12.320.47).

5. See also 3.182-190, especially the Brahmans' self-praise, 3.182.19-23.

6. The literature on the *Bhagavad-gītā* is very extensive. A partial summary can be found in Pusalker, *op. cit.*, pp. 163-87.

7. See Franklin Edgerton, *The Bhagavad-gītā,* Part II, Harvard Oriental Series 39 (Cambridge, Mass., 1944), p. 19.

8. A good edition and translation of this book is R. P. Kangle, *The Kauṭiliya Arthaśātra,* 3 vols. (Univ. of Bombay, 1960-65).

9. See Richard Garbe, *Die Sāṃkhya Philosophie* (Leipzig: H. Haessel, 1917), pp. 118-41, for a review of these theories. Erich Frauwallner, *Geschichte der Indischen Philosophie,* 2 vols. (Salzburg and Vienna; Otto Müller, 1953), pp. 97-146, distinguishes three stages of development in Epic thinking. See also Arthur Berriedale Keith, *The Sāṃkhya System* (Calcutta: Association Press, n.d.), pp. 27-53.

10. The *guṇas* are described in 3.203.1-12; 12.301.15-16, and *passim.* Their colors (white, red, and black) are given in 12.291.45.

11. This notion is found in the *Bhagavad-gītā.*

12. See the bibliography in Garbe, *op. cit.,* pp. 105-12. See also Edward Hamilton Johnston, *The Early Sāṃkhya* (London: The Royal Asiatic Society, 1937); Pulinbihari Chakravarti, *Origin and Development of the Sāṃkhya System of Thought,* Calcutta Sanskrit Series No. 30 (Calcutta: Metropolitan Printing and Publishing House, 1951); and V. M. Bedekar, "The Development of the Sāṃkhya and the Problem of the Sastitantra," *Journ. of the Univ. of Poona* 11 (1959), pp. 37-49. All these works deal with the epic Sāṃkhya in a historical perspective. The only attempts to describe the *Mahābhārata* Sāṃkhya *per se,* are Frauwallner *op. cit.,* and especially F. Edgerton, "The Meaning of Sāṅkhya and Yoga," *Am. J. of Philology* 45 (1924) 1-46. Classical Sāṃkhya recognizes 25 basic elements; 5 gross elements, 5 sense objects, 5 sense organs, 5 organs of actions, a *manas,* an *ahaṃkāra,* a *buddhi,* a *puruṣa* and a *prakṛti.* In the Epic they vary in number from 18 to 31.

Chapter Six

1. Quoted from the Sambhava Jātaka; see E. B. Cowell ed., *The Jātakas,* translated by various scholars, *vol.* V, translated by H. T.

Francis, 2nd ed. (London: Pali Text Society, Luzac and Co., 1957), *Jātaka* No. 515. Other references are in H. Lüders, "Die Jātakas und die Epik," *Philologica Indica,* pp. 80-106.

2. *Ibid., Kunala Jātaka,* No. 536.

3. *Ibid., Kumbha Jātaka,* No. 512.

4. See Edward Hamilton Johnston, ed. and trans., *The Buddhacarita,* by Aśvaghosa, Panjab University Oriental Publications Nos. 31 and 32, 2 vols. (Calcutta: Baptist Mission Press, 1935 and 1936), especially the introduction to Part II, pp. xvi-xvii.

5. Juthika Ghosh, *Epic Sources of Sanskrit Literature,* Calcutta Sanskrit College Research Series XXIII (Calcutta, 1963), gives a much fuller account.

6. Edited and translated by C. R. Devadhar, *Nine Plays Attributed to Bhāsa* (Poona: Oriental Book Agency), 1957-62.

7. Numerous translations exist, of which the most faithful is Murray B. Emeneau, trans., *Kālidāsa's Abhijñāna-śakuntalā* (Berkeley: Univ. of California Press, 1962). References to editions and translations can be found there, p. viii.

8. Edited by J. V. Bhaṭṭācārya, *Kirātārjunīyam,* by Bhāravi (Calcutta: Vīdan Press, 1875). Translated into German by Carl Cappeller, *Bharavi's poem Kiratarjuniya,* Harvard Or. Ser. 15 (Cambridge, Mass., 1912).

9. Edited by Kāśināth Pāṇḍurang Parab and Dhuṇḍi P. Vajhe, *Harṣacarita* (Bombay: Nirnayasagara Press, 1892), and with notes by Pāṇḍurang V. Kane, *Harṣacarita* (Bombay: Nirnayasagara Press, 1917). It was translated by E. B. Cowell and F. W. Thomas, *The Harṣacarita of Bāṇa,* Oriental Translation Fund New Series II (London, 1897).

10. A detailed exposition of these quotations is found in W. Cartillieri, "Das Mahābhārata bei Subandhu und Bāṇa," *Wiener Zeitschrift f.d. Kunde d. Morgenlandes* 13 (1899), pp. 57-74.

11. Edited by Hari N. Apte and others, *Śrimadbhagavad gītā with Śaṅkara's Commentary* (in Sanskrit) (Poona: Ānandāśrama Sanskrit Series No. 34, 1908). Translated by A. Mahādeva Śāstri, *The Bhagavad-gītā with the Commentary of Śrī Saṅkarāchārya,* 2nd ed. (Mysore, 1901).

12. Edited by the Pandits Durgāprasāda and Sivadatta, *The Sisupalavadha,* 7th ed. (Bombay: Nirnaya Sagara Press, 1917).

13. See Cartillieri, *op. cit.,* pp. 57-58.

14. Edited with English notes by Nārāyaṇa Bālakrishṇa Godabole, *The Veṇisamhara by Bhatta Nārāyaṇa* (in Sanskrit) (Poona: Vṛtta Prasāraka Press, 1867).

15. Instructive as to its modern appreciation are the comments of

S. K. De, who calls the drama "graceless, unrefined, not well-executed" and Bhīma "a boisterous, ferocious savage." See S. N. Dasgupta and S. K. De, *A History of Sanskrit Literature,* 2nd ed. (Calcutta: Univ. of Calcutta, 1962), Vol. I, pp. 275-76.

16. Edited by Pandit Śivadatta, *Śrīharsha's Naishadhīyacharita,* 6th ed. (Bombay: Nirnaya-sagar Press, 1928). Translated by Krishna K. Handiqui, *Naiṣadhacarita of Śrīharsa,* 2nd ed., Deccan College Monograph Series 14 (Poona, 1956).

17. *Dhvanyāloka,* Bk. IV, which is not available to me. See V. Raghavan, *The Number of Rasas* (Madras: Adyar, 1940), who paraphrases stirringly: "If one finds relish and importance in the subsidiary themes of marriage, dice, suffering, fight, it does not prevent another reader of nobler instincts and mystic disposition, seeing through these and deducing the greatness of the Lord, of Dharma, Śama and Mokṣa." (p. 32).

18. Edited by Peter Peterson, *Hitopadeśa by Nārāyaṇa Bhaṭṭa* (Bombay, 1887). Translated many times, e.g., Francis Johnson, rev. by L. D. Barnett (London, 1928).

19. See Ludwik Sternbach, *The Hitopadeśa and Its Sources* (Baltimore, American Oriental Society, 1960). The count is mine.

20. Edited by the Pandits Durgāprasāda and Śivadatta, *The Kathāsaritsāgara of Somadevabhaṭṭa,* 4th ed. (Bombay: Nirnayasāgar Press, 1930). Translated by Charles H. Tawney, *The Kathāsaritsāgara,* 2 vols. (Calcutta: Bibl. Indica, 1880-84), and in Penzer's great work: N. M. Penzer ed., *The Ocean of Story,* 10 vols. (London: [Privately published] 1924-28).

21. See Pandurang V. Kane, *History of Dharmaśāstra,* 5 vols. (Poona: Bhandarkar Or. Res. Inst., 1930-62), Vol. I, pp. 151-55, where references can be found to earlier investigations of the relationship between Manu and the *Mahābhārata.*

22. Edited by Vasudeva Sarman, *Manusmṛti* (in Sanskrit), 6th ed. (Bombay: Nirnaya-sagara Press, 1920). Translated by Georg Bühler, *The laws of Manu,* Sacred Books of the East No. 25 (Oxford Univ. Press, 1886), and with a very elaborate commentary and cross-references by Gangānātha Jhā, *Manusmṛti,* 5 vols. of Translation, 3 vols. of Notes (Calcutta: Univ. of Calcutta, 1920-29).

23. See Kangle, *op. cit.,* Vol. III, pp. 6-7.

24. Edited by S. Pandurang, *Śrīmadbhāgavatam* (Bombay: Nirnayasagara Press, 1950). Translated in the *Kalyāṇakalpataru,* ed. anon. "Bhāgavatamahāpurāṇa", text and translation (Gorakhpur: Gita Press, 1952-59). Other *Purāṇas* that have borrowed from the *Mahābhārata* are the *Brahma-purāṇa,* the *Matsya-purāṇa,* the *Padma-purāṇa* (see Shripad Krishna Belvalkar, "The Cosmographical Epi-

sode in the Mahābhārata and the Padmapurāṇa," in *A Vol. of Eastern and Indian Studies Presented to Prof. F. W. Thomas* [Bombay, 1939] pp. 19-28, and the literature there), the *Kūrma-purāṇa, Skandapurāṇa Varāha-purāṇa, Vāyu-purāṇa, Viṣṇu-purāṇa* and *Viṣṇudharmottara-purāna,* and the *Harivaṃśa;* see *V. S. Sukthankar, Āraṇyakaparvan* (Poona: Bhandarkar Or. Res. Inst., 1942), p. XIV.

25. P. E. Dumont, ed. and trans., *L'Īśvaragītā,* texte extrait du Kūrma-Purāṇa (Baltimore, 1933).

26. See Helmuth von Glasenapp, *Madhva's Philosophie* (Bonn and Leipzig: K. Schroeder Verlag, 1923), pp. 8ff.

27. The legends are summarized by Ernst Leumann, "Beziehungen der Jaina-literatur zu anderen Literaturkreisen Indiens," *Proc. 6th International Congress of Orientalists* (Leiden, 1883), Part III, Sec. 2, pp. 469-564, particularly on pp. 541-51. An excellent summary of Jain literature is Maurice Winternitz, *History of Indian Literature* (Calcutta: Univ. of Calcutta, 1933), Vol. II, pp. 424-595.

28. See Mironow, *op. cit.,* pp. 29ff.

29. Partly edited by Muni Charanvijaya, *Triṣaṣṭiśalākāpuruṣa-caritram,* 2 vols. (Bhāvnagar: Śrī-Jaina-Ātmananda-Sabhā, 1936 and 1950). Vol. I contains Book I, Vol. II, Books III-IV. The work has been translated by Helen M. Johnson, *Triṣaṣṭiśalākāpuruṣacaritra of Hemacandra,* 6 vols. (Baroda: Oriental Institute, 1931-62). The incidents described are from Bk. VIII of Johnson's translation.

30. Translated by Charles H. Tawney, *Kathākoça,* Oriental Translation Fund N.S.6 (London, 1895).

31. Presumably, many of the stories related do not originate in our *Mahābhārata,* but in folk tales.

32. A general survey of modern Indian literature can be found in Suniti Kumar Chatterji, *Languages and Literatures of Modern India* (Calcutta: Bengal Publishers, 1963).

33. See Mayadhar Mansinha, *History of Oriya Literature* (New Delhi: Sahitya Akademi, 1962). A recent edition is by the Rādhāramaṇa Pustakālaya (Cuttack: Orissa, 1958).

34.See Dinesh Chandra Sen, *History of Bengali Language and Literature* (Calcutta: Univ. of Calcutta, 1911), and ibid., *Selections from Bengali Literature,* 2 vols. (Calcutta, 1914).

35. Sen calls this incident "a masterpiece of tender faith" (*History,* p. 217).

36. See Banikanta Kakati, *Aspects of Early Assamese Literature* (Gauhati, 1953).

37. See P. T. Raju, *Telugu Literature* (Bombay: The International Book House, 1944) and Narasimha Acharya, "The Āndhra Mahābhāratamu," *A.B.O.R.I.* 22 (1941), pp. 97-102.

38. See D. L. Narasiṃhachar, "Old Kannaḍa Literature," in *Karnataka Darshana, Volume Presented to R. R. Diwakar* (Bombay, 1955), pp. 90-115.

39. Narasiṃhachar adds: ". . . his (Karṇa's) anxiety to keep himself pure and truthful under the most exacting circumstances do (does) draw out the sighs and tears of any of us and in his exalted death we feel a pang in the heart." (*op.cit.,* p. 97).

40. See R. Y. Dharwadkar, "Medieval Kannaḍa Literature," in *Karnataka Darshana, Volume Presented to R. R. Diwakar* (Bombay, 1955), pp. 115-30.

41. See S. V. Ranganna, "Folk Literature of Karnatak," *ibid.,* pp. 146-60.

42. See *The Cultural Heritage of India,* 3 vols., 2nd rev. and enlarged ed. (Calcutta: Ramakrishna Mission Institute of Culture, 1953-62), Vol. II, pp. 112-13.

43. See George Coedès, *Les états hindouisés de l'Indochine et Indonésie* (Paris: E. de Boccard, 1948), p. 70. Kauṇḍinya is mentioned once in the *Mbhr.* (2.4.14).

44. See K. Bhattacharya, *Les religions brahmaniques dans l'ancien Cambodge, d'après l'épigraphie et l'iconographie* (Paris: École Française d'Extrême Orient, Vol. 49, 1961), p. 12.

45. See Thao Pouvong, *Initiation á la littérature laotienne* (Paris: École Française d'Extrême Orient, 1948-49).

46. Himanshu Bhusan Sarkar, *Indian Influences on the Literature of Java and Bali* (Calcutta: Greater India Society, 1934), presents a good survey of Hindu-Javanese literature.

47. For this quotation from the *Rāmāyaṇa,* see D. R. Mankad, *Kiṣkindhākānda,* Vol. IV of the critical edition of the *Vālmiki-Rāmāyaṇa* (Baroda: Oriental Institute, 1965).

48. See *Epigraphia Indica* XVII (1923-24), pp. 323 and 326.

49. On Java, for example, are mountains named Meru, Arjuna, Bràmà (Brahma), etc.

50. I go by a statement in R. Ng. Poerbatjaraka and C. Hooykaas, trans., "Bhārata-Yuddha," by Mpu Sedah and Mpu Panuluh, *Djawa* 14 (1934), p. VIIIa.

51. See H. Neubronner van der Tuuk and H. Kern, "Inhoudsopgave van het Mahābhārata in 't Kawi," *Tijdschrift voor Indische Taal-, Landen Volkenkunde* (from here on cited as *TLV*), 3d Series, Vol. VI (1871), pp. 92-95. Belvalkar erroneously concludes that the Javanese order differed from the Indian (S. K. Belvalkar, *The Āśramavāsikaparvan* [Poona: Bhandarkar Oriental Inst., 1959], Introduction, p. xxix). The Javanese MSS are corrupt, but the Sanskrit order of the *parvans* can be reconstructed from the summary descrip-

tion of contents, Van der Tuuk, *op. cit.,* p. 94. For Belvalkar's reference to Lévi, read (p. xxxiii) : "at the end of the 10th century . . ."

52. The editions are: *Ādiparva* (one chapter only) by Hendrik Kern, "De Oudjavaansche vertaling van 't Mahābhārata," *Verh. der Kon. Ak. van Wetenschappen, Afd. Letterkunde XI* (1877), 29 pages, Dutch translation; complete by Hendrik H. Juynboll ed., *Ādiparwa, Oudjavaansch prozageschrift* (Den Haag: Nijhoff, 1906). *Virāṭaparva* by H. H. Juynboll ed., *Wirāṭaparwa* (Den Haag, 1912), and partly, with Dutch translation by Abraham A. Fokker, *Wirāṭaparwa I* (Den Haag: Leiden Univ. Diss., 1938). The *Udyogaparva* is very corrupt; see H. H. Juynboll, "De verhouding van het Oudjavaansche Udyogaparwa tot zijn Sanskṛt origineel," *TLV* 69 (1914), pp. 219-96. *Bhīṣmaparva* by Jan Gonda ed., "Het Oud-Javaansche Bhīṣmaparwa," *Bibliotheca Javanica* 7 (1936), and "Aantekeningen," *ibid.,* 7A (1937). The *Āśramavasana, Mausala-* and *Prasthānikaparvans* were published together, with a Dutch translation, by H. H. Juynboll, *Drie Boeken van het Oud-Javaansche Mahābhārata* (Den Haag: Leiden Diss., 1893). The *Bhagavad-gītā* was published separately by Jan Gonda, "The Javanese Version of the Bhagavad-gītā," *TLV* 75 (1935), pp. 36-82. See also Belvalkar, *The Bhīṣmaparvan* (Poona: Bhandarkar O.R.I., 1947), pp. xcii-cii.

53. See G. A. J. Hazeu, "Het Oud-Javaansche Adiparwa en zijn Sankṛt-origineel," *TLV* 44 (1901), p. 290.

54. Edited by J. G. H. Gunning, *Bhārata-Yuddha* (Den-Haag: Nijhoff, 1903), the Old Javanese text. Translated into Dutch by Poerbatjaraka and Hooykaas, *op. cit.* (See note 50.)

55. Edited and translated by A. B. Cohen-Stuart, "Brata-Joeda, Indisch Javaansch Heldendicht," *Lembaga Kebudajaan Indonesia,* formerly *Verhandelingen van het Bataviaasch Genootschap van Kunsten en Wetenschappen* (hereafter cited as *VBG*) XXVII (trans.) and XXVIII (1860).

56. Gonda claims that this betrayal is suggested by the language of the Old Javanese *Bhārata-Yuddha* also, but it cannot be traced to the Old Javanese *Mahābhārata,* because the *Karṇa-parva* is unavailable. See Jan Gonda, "Het verraad van Salya in het Bhārata—Yuddha," *TBG* 72 (1932), pp. 596-617.

57. See, esp., H. Neubronner van der Tuuk, "Geschiedenis der Pandawas naar een Maleis handschrift," *Tijdschrift v. h. Bat. Gen. v. K. en W.,* 21 (1874), 1-90 and *id.,* "Eenige Maleische Wajangverhalen toegelicht," *TLV* 25 (1879), pp. 489-537. The incident of the burning of the gum house is found in Hendrik Kern, "Obongobongan bale si galagala," *Verh, Kon. Ak. Wet., Afd. Lettk. IX* (1877), 46 pages (Dutch).

58. Edited and translated into Dutch by R. Ng. Poerbatjaraka, "Arjuna-Wiwāha," *TLV* 82 (1926), pp. 181-305.

59. The purpose of the composition of the *Arjuna-vivāha* was either to celebrate Airlañga's marriage to a Sumatran princess (so C. C. Berg, "De Arjunawiwāha, Er-langga's levensloop en bruiloftslied?" *TLV* 97 [1938], pp. 19-94), or to glorify his relationship to his half-sister from East Java (so Ir. J. L. Moens, "De stamboom van Airlangga," *TLV* 84 [1950-51], pp. 110-59).

60. See J. L. A. Brandes, *Beschrijving van de ruine bij de desa Toempang genaamd Tjandi Djago,* Archaeologisch Onderzoek van Nederlandsch-Indie," Vol. I (Den Haag, 1904), plates 194-75 (sic).

61. See A. J. Bernet-Kempers, *Ancient Indonesian Art* (Amsterdam: C. J. van der Peet, 1959), plate 192.

62. See Van der Tuuk, *op. cit.,* 1879, who describes many unusual *wayang* adaptations.

63. See Hendrik Kern, *op. cit.,* 1877, p. 8.

64. See Bishop G. E. Moule, "A Buddhist Sheet Tract," *J. of the China Branch Royal Asiatic Society XIX,* Part I (1884), pp. 94-102, which also shows a sketch of the man in the well.

65. R. G. Harshe, "The Arabic Version of the Mahābhārata Legend," *BDCRI* II (1941), pp. 314-24, gives an English translation of the French translation by Reinaud, which is unavailable to me.

66. A translation of the *Mausala-parvan* is given by Major David Price, *The Last Days of Krishna and the Sons of Pandu,* Oriental Transl. Fund No. 1 (London, 1831), 75 pages.

67. See W. W. Tarn, *The Greeks in Bactria and India,* 2nd ed. (Cambridge, England, 1951), p. 376.

68. The inscription reads:
trini amuta padāni(su) anuṭhitāni nayaṃti svaga dama chāga apramāda "Three immortal precepts, if practised, lead to heaven: Restraint, Renunciation and Caution." The last part is *Mbhr.* 11.7.19c: *damas tyāgo 'pramādaś ca,* which are called "Brahma's three horses." For an account of this inscription, see H. C. Raychaudhri, "The Mahābhārata and the Besnagar Inscription of Heliodorus, *JASB NS* 18 (1922), pp. 269-71.

69. Sören Sörensen, *An Index to the Names of the Mahābhārata,* 2nd ed. (reprint) (Delhi: Motilal Banarsidass, 1963), *s.v.*

70. See Tarn, *op. cit. p. 379.* His reference is to Dio Chrysostomos LIII, 6.

71. *Mbhr.* 2.28.49. See also Franklin Edgerton, "Rome and (?) Anṭioch in the Mahābhārata," *JAOS* 58 (1938), pp. 262-65.

72. See Madeleine Lallemand, "Une source de l'Énéide: le Mahā-

bhārāta," *Latomus* 18 (1959), pp. 262-87, who lists these and other parallels.

73. See J. Leclant, "Reflets de l'Egypte dans la littérature latin," *Revue des Etudes Latines* 36 (1959), p. 82.

74. Translated by Douglas Ainslie, *John of Damascus,* 4th ed. (London, 1906).

75. Edited by Hermann Oesterley, *Gesta Romanorum* (Berlin, 1871) [in Latin]. The translation is mine.

76. See Laudedeo Testi, *Parma* (Bergamo: Instituto Italiano d'Arti Grafiche (1905)) [in Italian], p. 67. He claims that the French version of the story was used, but from Jean Soret, *Le Roman de Barlaam et Josaphat,* 2 vols. (Paris: Ed. J. Vrin, 1949-52), Vol. I, it is nor clear which one. Testi states that the legend is also portrayed in the San Marco in Venice (p. 67).

77. So already Ernst Kuhn, "Der Mann im Brunnen," in *Festgrusz an Otto von Böhtlingk* (Stuttgart, 1888), pp. 68-76.

78. See Paul Pelliot, *Notes on Marco Polo II* (Paris: Imprimerie Nationale, 1963), pp. 750-52. The Jesuit Mission at the Katsura Seminary published the legend in the Sanctos no Gosagueo, an abridgment of the *Acta Sanctorum,* in 1591.

79. See David Marshall Lang, *The Balavariani* (Berkeley; University of California, 1966), p. 10.

Chapter Seven

1. The early history of Sanskrit scholarship in the West is described by Winternitz, *HIL,* I, pp. 8-21.

2. Examples are Joh. H. Becker, *Mahābhārata, der grosze Krieg* (Berlin, 1888), Elisabeth Hering, *Savitrī* (Leipzig: Prisma Verlag, 1959), and Garret Holme, *Nanda, a Grove Play* (San Francisco: Bohemian Club, 1928).

3. See the very brief statement by Kurt F. Leidecker, "The Bhagavad-gītā and the St. Louis movement," *JAOS* Proc. 56 (1936), p. 415.

4. See Jean Herbert, *La mythologie hindoue—son message.* (Paris: Éditions Albin Michel, 1953). His translations are very unreliable.

5. *Cult, Her.,* II, p. 117.

6. See Heinrich Robert Zimmer, *The Art of Indian Asia* (New York: Pantheon, 1955) Vol. I, p. 167.

7. Zimmer, *op. cit.,* pp. 275-76.

8. See Vincent A. Smith, *History of Fine Art in India and Ceylon* (Oxford: Clarendon, 1911), p. 329.

9. See Mulk Raj Anand, *The Hindu View of Art* (Bombay: Asia Publishing House [n.d., 195?]), plate on pp. 28-19. Jarāsaṃdha, lying prostrate on the ground, has his feet encircled by Bhīma's mighty arms. Bhīma's left foot is about to break Jarāsaṃdha's back (unlike the Epic account), while Kṛṣṇa encourages him smilingly, his fists balled.

10. The stories are from *Sūr Sāgar of Sūr Dās,* 2 Vols., publ. by the Sūr Samiti (Benares, 1963).

11. From Rabindranath Tagore, *The Fugitive* (London: Mac-Millan and Co., 1921), pp. 173-94.

12. See K. R. Srinivāsa Iyengar, *Indian Writing in English* (Bombay; Asia Publishing House, 1962), pp. 193ff.

13. Iyengar, *op. cit.,* p. 197.

14. Sir Aurobindo Ghose, *Sāvitrī, a Legend and a Symbol,* 2 vols. (Pondicherry, 1951). Quotations are from Vol. I.

15. An advertisement for an American picture reads: "A 20th century Draupadī takes birth in Hollywood!" The reference is to "What a Way to Go!" with Shirley Maclaine (20th Century Fox, 1964). Her free behavior with male friends can be considered licentious, so that here again, as in Buddhist literature, we find Draupadī upheld as an immoral example.

16. Quoted in Aileen D. Ross, *The Hindu Family in Its Urban Setting* (Oxford University Press, 1961), p. 117.

17. See G. Morris Carstairs, *The Twice-Born* (London: The Hogarth Press, 1957).

18. Carstairs, *op. cit.,* pp. 84ff.

19. See Donald A. McGavran, *Education and the Beliefs of Popular Hinduism* (Jubbulpore: Mission Press, 1935).

20. See Dr. Kurtkoti, "Influence of the Mahābhārata on Hindu Social Life," *ABORI* 19 (1938), pp. 1-9.

Selected Bibliography

PRIMARY SOURCES

(*Chronological Order*)

The Mahābhārata. An epic poem. Edited by the Pandits attached to the Education Committee, 5 vols. Calcutta, 1834-39. The *editio princeps,* or "Calcutta Edition."

Mahābhārata, with Nilakantha's commentary, ed. Ātmarāma Khāḍilkar. Bombay: Gaṇpat Kṛṣṇaji's Press, 1863. This is the "Bombay edition," in *poṭhi* form.

Srimanmahabharatam . . . , ed. T. R. Krishnacharya and T. R. Vyasacharya, 23 vols. Kumbakonam: Madhva Vilas Book Depot; Bombay: Nirṇayasagara Press, 1906-14. This is the "Kumbhakonam edition."

Mahābhārata, with Nīlakaṇṭha's commentary, ed. Ramachandra Sh. Kinjavadekar. Poona, 1929-33. The "Chitrashala edition."

The Mahābhārata (*Southern Recension*), ed. P.S.S. Sastri, 18 vols. Madras, 1931-36.

Mahābhārata, for the first time critically edited . . . , ed. Vishnu Sitaram Sukthankar, 19 vols. Poona: Bhandarkar Or. Research Inst., 1933-66. This is the "Critical Edition." Many different scholars edited the various volumes. After April 1943, S. K. Belvalkar became the General Editor.

SECONDARY SOURCES

1. Translations (chronological order)

FAUCHE, T., Trans. *Le Mahābhārata, poème épique,* 10 vols. Paris, 1863-70. The first complete translation up to the *Karṇa-parvan.* Fauche died before the remainder was finished.

ROY, PROTAP CHANDRA, ed. *The Mahābhārata,* 18 vols., trans. Kisari Mohan Ganguli. Calcutta: Bhārata Press, 1883-96. The translation is based on the Calcutta edition augmented by other manuscripts. It is a fascinating translation which the editor completed "in the fag end of the nineteenth century," as he terms it, at the expense of great personal hardship. He rarely sold the copies, but gave them away and died before it was completed. The tone of the translation is solemn and moralistic, its style Gothic and at times impressive. But as a translation it is not always reliable, since difficult passages are frequently rendered wrongly. Sometimes Roy inserts passages not found even in the Critical Edition. On the whole, it should be used with caution; as a source book for secondary studies it is untrustworthy. A second edition, omitting the śloka references appeared in Calcutta 1919-35 (11 vols.); it has recently been republished in Delhi: Oriental Publishing Co., n.d., in 12 vols. Selections from the first and second volumes have been published by S. C. Nott, ed., *The Mahābhārata,* London: Janus Press, 1956.

BALLIN, L., trans. *Le Mahābhārata.* IX Çalyaparva et Livres X, XI, XII, 2 vols. Paris: Ernest Leroux, 1899. A continuation of Fauche's translation.

DUTT, MANMATHA NATH, trans. *A Prose English Translation of the Mahābhārata,* 6 vols. Calcutta: H. C. Dass; 1895-1905.

KERBAKER, MICHELE, trans. *Il Mahābhārata,* 5 vols. Rome 1933-39. A free rendering of the *Mahābhārata* into ottava rima.

KAL'YANOVA, V. I., trans. *Makhabkharata. Ādiparvan,* Moscow and Leningrad: Ak. Nauk SSSR, 1950. This is the first translation of the Critical Edition into a Western Language. The work is being continued.

PISANI, VITTORE, trans. *Mahābhārata, episodi scelti,* Torino: Tipografia Sociale Torinese, 1954. A translation of a few episodes into Italian, with a good introduction.

SMIRNOVA, B. L., trans. *Makhabkharata. Sabkhaparvan,* Ashkhabad: Ak. Nauk Turkmenskoy, 1962. *Makhabkharata. Vanaparvan* [*sic*], *ibid.,* 1962. *Bkhagavadgīta., ibid.,* 1960. *Makhabkharata. Mokṣadharma, ibid.,* 1961. An account of Soviet studies relating to the *Mahābhārata* is given by N. Vishnevskaya "Mahābhārata—Ancient Indian Epic," *Journal of the Ganganatha Jha Research Society* 27 (1960-61), pp. 59-62.

Selections in English

ARNOLD, SIR EDWIN, *Indian Idylls.* London, 1883, A lyrical though somewhat archaically phrased set of translations.

AYYAR, JAGADISA. *The Mahā Bhārata.* Madras, 1922.

DUTT, ROMESH CHUNDER. *The Mahābhārata Condensed into English Verse.* London: J. M. Dent, 1898. A free condensation of the epic story, omitting most episodes. Reprinted many times, e.g., in the Modern Library Series.

JOHNSON, FRANCIS. *Selections from the Mahābhārata.* London. 1842. The earliest English translations from the *Mahābhārata.*

MACFIE, JOHN MANDEVILLE. *The Mahābhārata: A Summary.* Christian Literary Society for India, Madras, 1921.

MUKHOPADHAY, S. C. *The Mahābhārata, Translated into English Prose with Esoteric Commentary.* Calcutta, 1899. One of the many works interpreting the Mahābhārata as a work of theosophical value.

NARASIMHAN, V. *The Mahābhārata,* English version based on selected verses. New York: Columbia Univ. Press, 1965. The first English abridgment based on the Critical Edition, quite faithful to the text. It gives the Epic story but omits the episodes.

OMAN, J. C. *Struggles in the dawn: The Stories of the Great Indian Epics.* Lahore, 1893.

RAJAGOPALACHARI, C. *Mahābhārata.* Bombay: Bharatiya Vidya Bhavan, 1950. Many reprints. It is a translation from his Tamil summary of *Mahābhārata* stories (publ. 1943) which in turn was based on the free Tamil translation from the Sanskrit original. In India it is a very popular work, but owing to its implied moral message and didactic phrasing, its value escapes many Westerners.

RICE, STANLEY. *Tales from the Mahābhārata.* London, 1924.

SEEGER, ELIZABETH. *The Five Brothers.* New York, 1948. A reworking of the epic story, based on Ganguli's translation.

SRINIVASA-RAO, C. V. *Mahābhārata,* 3 vols. Bangalore, 1956-61. Also based on Ganguli's translation.

SUBRAMANIAM, KAMALA. *Mahābhārata.* Bombay: Bharatiya Vidya Bhavan, 1965. Useful index of names. Quite comprehensive and rather colloquial in style.

2. Indexes and Summaries

DOWSON, J. A. *A Classical Dictionary of Hindu Mythology and Religion, Geography, History and Literature.* London: Trübner Oriental Series, 1879; reprinted many times. A useful reference for the quick identification of mythological names.

JACOBI, HERMANN. *Mahābhārata. Inhaltsangabe, Index und Concordanz.* Bonn: Friedrich Cohen, 1903. A very complete and reliable summary of contents of every chapter. It distinguishes the moralistic from the narrative and episodic chapters.

RICE, E. P. *Analysis and Index of the Mahābhārata.* London: Oxford Univ. Press, 1934. Rather too brief a summary, it is useful for its Index of Subjects.

SÖRENSEN, SÖREN. *An Index of the Names in the Mahābhārata.* London, 1904-25; reprinted, Delhi: Motilal Banarsiass, 1963. An excellent index of proper names, quite exhaustive, giving the names of places, people, as well as their eponyms, with cross-references to the numerous epithets by which they are known in the *Mahābhārata,* in the Western alphabetical order. The work also contains genealogical tables and summaries of episodes. All text references are to both Bombay and Calcutta editions.

WINTERNITZ, MAURICE. *History of Indian Literature,* Vol. I. Calcutta: Univ. of Calcutta, 1963, pp. 273-389. This is a general, but quite adequate account furnished with numerous bibliographical references up to about 1925.

3. Scholarly Publications

ABORI, Annals of the Bhandarkar Oriental Research Institute. Poona, 1920-. This journal is almost exclusively devoted to text-critical and other technical problems of the Critical Edition.

AUTRAN, CHARLES. *L'épopée indoue.* Paris, 1946. This is a comparative study of the *Mahābhārata* with the Greek epics and also its relation to the Near Eastern cultural setting.

EDGERTON, FRANKLIN. *The Beginnings of Indian Philosophy.* London: Allen and Unwin, 1965. A number of important, new translations from the *Mokṣadharma,* as well as parts of his earlier translation of the *Bhagavad-gītā.*

———— "E, W. Hopkins 1857-1932," *JAOS* 52 (1932). A summary of the most important publications by E. Washburn Hopkins, many of which deal with the *Mahābhārata.*

FAUSBOLL, MICHAEL VIGGO. *Indian Mythology according to the Mahābhārata.* London: Luzac and Co., 1902. A rather incomplete, yet useful description of Epic mythological characters using direct quotations from the Sanskrit text.

FRAUWALLNER, ERICH. *Geschichte der Indichen Philosophie,* 2 vols. Salzburg and Vienna: Otto Muller, 1953. Contains a section on Epic philosophy. See above, Chapter 5, note 9.

GHOSH, JUTHIKA. *Epic Sources of Sanskrit Literature.* Calcutta, 1963. A comprehensive account of titles of Sanskrit works inspired by the *Rāmāyaṇa* and the *Mahābhārata.*

HOLTZMANN, ADOLF. *Das Mahābhārata im Osten und Westen.* Kiel, 1895. The last part of his tetralogy on the *Mahābhārata,* it deals with the relationship of the Epic to other Sanskrit works and those of the West.

HOPKINS, EDWARD WASHBURN, *Epic Mythology,* Grundriss der Indo-Arischen Philologie . . . Vol. I:4, Strassburg: Karl Trübner, 1915. Describes the mythology of the *Mahābhārata and Rāmāyaṇa* very thoroughly, often with references. A good work.

———. *The Great Epic of India.* New York: Charles Scribner's Sons, 1902. By far the most authoritative work on the *Mahābhārata's* origin, history, and versification. Many of his conclusions have been preempted by the *Mahābhārata's* Critical Edition, yet his studies are still of great importance. Only his views on the philosophy of the Epic have not been supported by other authors.

———. "The Social and Military Position of the Ruling Caste. . . . ," *Journ. of the Am. Or. Soc.* 13 (1889) 57-376. This article contains a wealth of information on military and social questions, such as battle orders, strategy, armament, the status of the castes and of women, and so forth.

KANE, PANDURANG V. *History of Dharmaśāstra,* 5 vols. Poona: Bhandarkar Or. Res. Inst., 1930-62. The *Mahābhārata* is quoted frequently in this work in connection with Kane's comparative studies on Indian law. References to sacrifices, observances, customs, places of pilgrimage, and the like, may be found here.

LAW, BIMALA CHURN. *Historical Geography of Ancient India.* Paris: Soc. Asiatique de Paris, 1954. This work should be used with caution, since the identifications of places, rivers, and mountains are very tentative.

POTTER, KARL H. *Presuppositions of India's Philosophies,* Englewood Cliffs, N.J.: Prentice Hall, 1963. Describes the mutual relationships of the various branches of philosophy.

PUSALKER, A. D. *Studies in the Epics and Purāṇas.* Bombay: Bhavan's Book University, Bharatiya Vidya Bhavan, 1955. On pp. 112-62 there is an annotated bibliography of works relating to the *Mahābhārata* published between 1925 and 1955.

SUKTHANKAR, VISHNU S. *Sukthankar Memorial Edition,* Vol. I, ed. P. K. Gode, Bombay: Karnatak Publishing House, 1944. All Sukthankar's articles on the *Mahābhārata,* with the exception of the work below, have been collected in this publication. The "Prolegomena" to the *Adiparvan* (pp. I-CX) is a succinct and thoughtful evaluation of the *Mahābhārata's* text-critical status.

———. *On the Meaning of the Mahābhārata.* Bombay: Asiatic Society, 1957. A criticism of Western appreciations of the Epic and an explanation of its metaphysical and philosophical significance.

VAIDYA, CHINTAMĀNA V. *Epic India.* Bombay, 1907. An attempt to extract historical and social information from the *Mahābhārata* and, like most works of its kind, not very convincing.

WINTERNITZ, MAURICE. *History of Indian Literature,* Vol. I, pp. 273-417, Calcutta: Univ. of Calcutta, 1963, pp. 273-77. Here the relationship of the Epic to earlier Sanskrit works is described. On the whole, this problem is obscure.

4. *The Bhagavad-gītā*

DIVANJI, P. C. *Critical Word-Index to the Bhagavad-gītā.* Bombay: New Book Company, 1946. It gives an alphabetical listing of the words and their meanings.

EDGERTON, FRANKLIN. *Bhagavad-gīta,* 2 vols. Harvard Or. Ser. No. 38 and 39. Cambridge: Harvard Univ. Press, 1944. Part I has the transliterated Sanskrit text with the translation facing each page. Part II contains an interpretation and Sir Edwin Arnold's verse translation: "The Song Celestial." It is the best literal English translation.

HILL, W. D. P. *The Bhagavad-gītā.* Oxford, 1928. A good translation with an introductory discussion of the Kṛṣṇa cult.

JACOB, COLONEL GEORGE ADOLPHUS. *A Concordance to the Principal Upaniṣads and Bhagavad-gītā.* Bombay, 1891. It lists the quarter ślokas in the Devanāgarī script.

PUSALKER, A. D. *Op. cit.* pp. 163-178, has a comprehensive bibliography of articles published on the *Bhagavad-gītā* up to 1955.

RADHAKRISHNAN, SARVEPALLI. *The Bhagavadgītā.* London: Allen and Unwin, 1948. The transliterated text and a translation with a Vedāntic interpretation of the poem. Hindus set great store by this translation.

WINTERNITZ, MAURICE. *Op. cit.,* 374ff., lists translations and scholarly articles, as well as arguments for its dating, up to about 1925.

Glossary

Abhimanyu	Arjuna's son by his wife Subhadrā, Kṛṣṇa's sister. He became the grandfather of Janamejaya.
Agastya	A holy sage.
Agni	The god of fire, one of the guardians of the quarters.
Ambā	Daughter of the king of Benares and abducted by Bhīṣma during her *svayaṃvara*. Reborn as Śikhaṇḍinī she was transformed into a man, Śikhaṇḍin.
Apsaras	Name of a class of heavenly nymphs.
Arjuna	Third of the five Pāṇḍava brothers, the most valorous of all. He was the son of Indra by Kuntī and married Draupadī and Subhadrā. He is often represented as an ascetic.
Asvatthāman	Droṇa's son, a warrior on the Kuru side and one of the three surviving Kurus.
Aśvins	"Horsemen," twin gods, handsome heavenly physicians, fathers of Nakula and Sahadeva.
Balarāma	Kṛṣṇa's elder brother, a noncombatant.
Bhagīratha	A king who practiced penance to cause the Ganges to come to earth.
Bharata	Son of Śakuntalā and Duḥṣanta and the supposed ancestor of Vicitravirya, the nominal father of both Pāṇḍavas and Kurus.
Bhīma (sena)	Second of the five Pāṇḍava brothers, son of Kuntī by Vāyu and father of Ghaṭotkaca by Hiḍimbā.
Bhīṣma	Counsellor to King Dhṛtarāṣṭra, son of Śāntanu by Gāngā. He is a symbol of wisdom, righteousness and selflessness, one of the key figures in the story.

Bhṛgu	One of the great Ṛṣis, ancestor of the Bhārgava clan of fire priests. They have been credited with rewriting the *Mahābhārata* emphasizing their own achievements.
Brahman (*m.*)	A god, identified with Prajāpati.
Bṛhannaḍā	Arjuna's name when he assumed service as a dancing instructor at Virāṭa's court.
Cedi	Name of the country of king Jayadratha.
Cyavana	A sage, who married a young girl and regained his youth.
Dadhīci	A sage.
Damayantī	Wife of Nala and heroine of the Nala-episode.
Dhanaṃjaya	"Winner of wealth," a name of Arjuna by which he is known in the *Jātakaṣ*.
Dhṛṣṭadyumna	Generalissimo of the Pāṇḍu army; the brother of Draupadī and king of the Pañcālas.
Dhṛtarāṣṭra	Father of the one hundred Kuru brothers; he was begotten by Vyāsa on Vicitravīrya's wife and married Gāndhārī. He is portrayed as an indecisive, blind old man.
Draupadī	Wife of the five Pāṇḍu brothers, also called Kṛṣṇa. Her humiliation at Dhṛtarāṣṭra's court led to the Pāṇḍavas' exile and the great battle was their revenge.
Droṇa	A tutor of both Pāṇḍavas and Kurus. He led the Kuru army from the eleventh to the fifteenth day and was ignominiously killed by Dhṛṣṭadyumna.
Drupada	King of Pañcāla, rather of Draupadī, enemy of Droṇa.
Duḥṣanta	A mythical king who seduced Śakuntalā.
Duḥśāsana	A son of Dhṛtarāṣṭra, Bhīma drank his blood in revenge for his insult to Draupadī.
Duryodhana	The Pāṇḍus' main antagonist, the eldest of Dhṛtarāṣṭra's one hundred sons. He was killed by Bhīma in a club fight.
Dvārakā	"City of Gates," Kṛṣṇa's capital, traditionally located on the Gujarātī coast.
Ekalavya	A poor Niṣāda boy who was forced to cut off his thumb to please Arjuna.

Gandhamādana	A forest where the Pāṇḍu brothers stayed.
Gāndhāri	Dhṛtarāṣṭra's good wife. She blindfolded herself to be blind like her husband.
Gandharva	Benevolent, heavenly musicians.
Gāṇḍīva	Arjuna's bow, a present from Agnī.
Gaṅgā	The River Ganges, mother of Bhīṣma.
Garuḍa	A divine bird of huge proportions, an enemy of snakes.
Ghaṭotkaca	Son of Bhīma's union with Hiḍimbā; a monster who assisted the Pāṇḍavas.
Hāstinapura	Capital of the Kuru country.
Hiḍimbā	An ogress; Bhīma's mistress for a year.
Indra	Ruler of the gods; also one of the guardians of quarters.
Indraprastha	Capital of the Pāṇḍus, where Yudhiṣṭhira established a palace and held a sacrifice.
Janamejaya	King of Hāstinapura who held a twelve year sacrifice during which the *Mahābhārata* was recited.
Jarāsaṃdha	A tyrannical king of Magadha who threatened to sacrifice one hundred captive kings, before he was killed by Bhīma.
Jayadratha	King of the Sindhus, son-in-law of Dhṛtarāṣṭra. He once abducted Draupadī.
Kāmboja	A kingdom to the northwest of India.
Kapila	A sage credited with the founding of the Sāṃkhya doctrine of philosophy.
Karṇa	Half-brother of Arjuna and Yudhiṣṭhira; an illegitimate son of Pṛthā by the Sun-god. He fights on the Kuru side and is killed by Arjuna.
Kaurava	"Inhabitant of Kuru country," the name of the enemies of the Pāṇḍus; also called Kurus.
Khāṇḍavaprastha	The land that the young Pāṇḍavas obtained as their patrimony, with Indraprastha as capital.
Kīcaka	A general at Virāṭa's court.
Kirāta	A hunter, or tribesman from the mountains.
Kṛpa	A warrior on the Kuru side, brother-in-law of Droṇa.
Kṛṣṇa	Arjuna's charioteer, and diplomatic emissary.

He revealed himself as a god in the *Bhagavad-gītā*.

Kṛtavarman — A warrior on the Pāṇḍus' side.

Kubera — Lord of the underworld and of wealth.

Kuntī — Also called Pṛthā. Mother of the three elder Pāṇḍu brothers, and of Karṇa.

Kuru — See Kaurava. The opponents of the Pāṇḍus in the war.

Kurukṣetra — "Field of the Kurus" was plain where the Great Battle was fought.

Lomaśa — A wandering sage.

Madra — A kingdom in Pakistan.

Mādrī — Pāṇḍu's second wife, mother of the twins by the Aśvins.

Magadha — A kingdom in eastern north India, present-day Bihar.

Mahādeva — A name for Śiva.

Mandara — A mountain used during the churning of the ocean.

Manu — The legendary first man.

Mathurā — Kṛṣṇa's city.

Matsya — A kingdom governed by Virāṭa.

Maya — The superhuman architect of Yudhiṣṭhira's palace.

Nahuṣa — Father of Yayāti. He was destroyed by his pride.

Nakula — The fourth of the Pāṇḍu brothers, son of Mādri by the Aśvin Nāsatya.

Nala — King of Niṣadha, hero of the Nala episode.

Nārada — A wandering sage.

Nārāyaṇa — A divine being, supreme god of a sect of Viṣṇu worshippers.

Niṣādas — A despised caste of lowly tribesmen.

Pāṇḍavas — The descendants of Pāṇḍu, also called Pāṇḍus. The name refers to the five brothers Yudhiṣthira, Bhīma, Arjuna, Nakula, and Sahadeva, or to their army opposing the Kurus, or Kauravas.

Pāṇḍu — Son of Vyāsa and Ambālikā, married to Kuntī and Mādrī. See Pāṇḍavas.

Parikṣit	Abhimanyu's son, who performed a snake sacrifice where the *Mahābhārata* was first recited.
Parāśara	Vyāsa's father who seduced a ferry-operator's daughter, Satyavatī.
Pāśupata	Arjuna's magic weapon.
Prajāpati	"Lord of creatures," an ancient god, identified with Brahman.
Pṛthā	See *Kuntī*.
Rākṣasa	A class of demons, ogres, giants, evil spirits.
Rāma	1. A great Bhṛgu hero, already retired at the time of the Great Battle. 2. Hero of the Rāma episode which is modeled after the *Rāmāyaṇa*.
Ṛṣi	An inspired poet, or visionary wise man.
Ṛśyaśṛṅga	A hermit boy whose seduction by a courtesan brought rain to the land of Vaṅga.
Sahadeva	Youngest of the Pāṇḍu brothers, son of Mādrī and an Aśvin.
Śakuni	The wicked brother of Gāndhārī and counsellor of Duryodhana. He defeated Yudhiṣṭhira in the gambling match.
Śakuntalā	Heroine of a romantic episode with Duḥṣanta, king of Kuru country.
Śālva	A king betrothed to Ambā.
Śalya	King of Madra, leader of the Kuru army on the last day of battle.
Saṃjaya	Dhṛtarāṣṭra's adviser and charioteer. He gained divine vision to report the battle events to the king.
Śikhaṇḍin(ī)	A warrior on the Pāṇḍu side, in a previous life a woman, Ambā. In the Javanese epic he becomes Arjuna's wife.
Śiśupāla	A cousin of Kṛṣṇa's and killed by the latter during Yudhiṣṭhira's sacrifice.
Śiva	An important, powerful god. Disguised as a Kirāta he fights with Arjuna over a boar.
Soma	The god of the moon.
Subhadrā	Kṛṣṇa's sister, abducted and married by Arjuna.
Sūrya	The god of the sun, father of Karṇa.

Sūta	The narrator of the *Mahābhārata.*
Takṣaka	King of the snakes, son of Kadrū.
Trigarta	Allies of the Kurus in their raid on Virāṭa's cattle.
Uśīnara	A pious king who saved a pigeon's life.
Vaiśaṃpāyana	A sage who learned the *Mahābhārata* from Vyāsa and recited it at Janamejaya's twelve-year sacrifice.
Varuṇa	The god of water, a guardian of the quarters.
Vāsuki	A king of the Nāgas, used by the gods and Asuras as a cord to churn the ocean.
Vāyu	The god of the wind, father of Bhīma.
Vicitravīrya	King of Hāstinapura, married to Ambikā and Ambālikā. He dies childless and in his stead Vyāsa begets his children, Dhṛtarāṣṭra and Pāṇḍu.
Vidura	Son of Vyāsa by a slave girl. He becomes Dhṛtarāṣṭra's counsellor and steadily pleads for peace.
Virāṭa	King of the Matsyas, near modern Jaipur, a friend and ally of the Pāṇḍus.
Viṣṇu	An important Epic god, glorified in the *Bhagavad-gītā.* Kṛṣṇa is regarded as his incarnation.
Vṛtra	A mythical demon, slain by Indra.
Vyāsa	"Arranger," the supposed composer of the *Mahābhārata* and the natural grandfather of both Pāṇḍu and Kuru factions.
Yakṣa	A class of mythical beings, dryads.
Yama	God of the dead and a guardian of the quarters.
Yamunā	A sacred river, now Jumnā.
Yayāti	A king of antiquity whose son Pūru was willing to assume the burden of his old age.
Yudhiṣṭhira	The eldest of the five Pāṇḍu brothers, son of Dharma; he is an epitome of righteousness.

Index

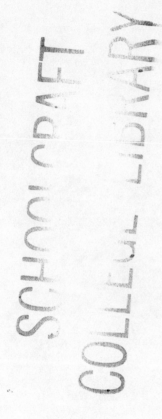